"This is a 'must rea[...] [...]
wedding! I've known Barba[...] [...] s
and in my opinion she is the [...] n
the country today on dressing mothers of th[...] id
groom! It is wonderful that someone this knowledgeable
is able to lay out, once and for all, everything that
mothers should know. She mixes so effectively sage
knowledge with so much humor! This is truly an
informative and fun read!"

Stephen N. Lang, CEO,
Mon Cheri Bridals

"It has been my distinct pleasure to work with
Barbara and her associates at T. Carolyn! She wields a
plethora of knowledge when it comes to dressing mothers
of the bride and groom—enabling each woman to choose
the perfect gown for her special event. She has that
peculiar skill to recognize which designs will enhance a
woman's beauty, and the ability to recognize what
changes or modifications are needed for a gown to bear
the signature mark of the woman wearing it.

"Throughout our business relationship, I have seen
that Barbara runs her store with extreme efficiency,
passion and integrity. Her continually striving for the
customer's happiness and satisfaction, in addition to her
business savvy, makes her a first rate businesswoman. I
am so pleased to have our gowns represented by T.
Carolyn, and recommend listening to any advice she has
in regard to this industry."

Kyle Yin, CEO,
Jasmine Bridal

"As a designer, I have longed for someone to create a handbook for mothers at the wedding. With so much misinformation readily available, someone needed to provide authoritative advice to mothers on how to look their best at their child's wedding. Thankfully, Barbara has now done so."

Ursula Garreau CEO,
Ursula of Switzerland

"I have learned so much from Barbara in her common sense approach to fashion."

Sharon Putnam,
Putnam Enterprises,
The Atlanta Apparel Mart

"Through the years my contact with Barbara has been solely on the phone. (She's in Houston and my company is in New York.) Yet, a voice speaks volumes of the substance of the person. She is a pleasure to work with because she knows exactly what works for her store and her customer and does not waste your time or her own. She is very professional and very human at the same time.

"There is no doubt that she knows her business inside and out and if there is anybody that can write a book for the Mother of the Bride or Groom, it is Barbara."

Elenitsa Damianou
DAMIANOU®

I WANT MY MOTHER'S DRESS TO MATCH THE NAPKINS

Funny Stories and Serious Advice
For Looking Your Best at Your Child's
Wedding

Barbara Coolidge Tibbetts

T.Carolyn Fashions is a registered trademark 2007

Cover designed by J. Dante Martin,
Global Marketing Solutions, Houston, Texas

ISBN: 1448673682
EAN-13: 9781448673681

A Handbook of
Fashion Advice for
Mothers of the Bride and Groom

Table of Contents

Dedication

To my late sister, Mary Beth Coolidge, J.D.

At a family dinner my then nine-year-old grandson, Dante, asked me how many pages were in my book. When I told him he then asked how long it had taken me to write the book. The look of amazement and consternation on his face and his reaction to my response were priceless as he remarked incredulously, "And it took you 15 *years*?!"

Preface

My decision to start writing this book came after my sister-in-law, who at the time was still living overseas, remarked that, since I was no longer teaching, she missed the wonderful and funny stories I used to tell about the experiences in my piano-teaching studio. Upon seeing my blank expression she asked, "You do remember those stories, don't you?" It was at that moment I realized that I didn't.

When I realized that most of the stories I'd been hearing in my store were probably not being remembered either, I rushed to the computer in my back office and began typing away. I frantically began trying to recall the wonderful things I had heard from customers in the past years, and thus *"I Want My Mother's Dress To Match The Napkins"* was born.

When I first began keeping track of the interesting things I was hearing as I worked with MOBs (mothers of the bride) and MOGs (mothers of the groom), I envisioned a book of cute and funny stories. However, the longer I worked with these women, the more convinced I became that a portion of my book needed to be a common sense approach to what really is important and what is nonsense. So, inevitably, this book has become a combination of both anecdotes and advice or, perhaps more accurately, advice with anecdotes often used to illustrate the advice presented.

In recounting the anecdotes in this book the intent was not to make fun of, or ridicule anyone, but to provide a realistic view of the problems and conflicts mothers face in choosing something to wear to the wedding. Its purpose is also to recount the lighter side of what, for many, is a very stressful experience. Uneventful weddings are rare occurrences. We go about our daily lives with a series of routines that we perform day after day and these routines are seldom subject to aberrations. Most of what we do today, we did yesterday, and the day before that, and the day before that, ad infinitum. Weddings, on the other hand, are rare and generally complex occurrences in each individual's life. And because of this, there is the potential for things not to go according to plans. Perhaps in reading this book each mother, bride or groom will realize that slip-ups and minor embarrassments are, to one degree or another, common to most if not all weddings. Perhaps, this will help ease the discomfort that some of you may have already experienced or will experience in the future.

In *every* culture weddings are supposed to be joyous events. They are a time of celebration. Sometime, we get so bogged down in details that minor things begin to seem major and we lose sight of what is really important. Over the past eighteen years, as I've worked with thousands of mothers, I've heard stories that were hilarious, stories that were sad, even some that were unbelievable. But, there was almost always a lesson to be learned.

Looking back on it all, I realize that my very first experience as a musician at a wedding actually set me up for authoring this book. I was twelve years old, in Port-of-

Spain, Trinidad, playing the organ for a wedding for the very first time. I was playing "Oh Perfect Love" prior to the groom's entrance, when an usher came up to me and whispered that the groom had forgotten the rings and I was to keep playing.

Being only twelve, and my first time to play at a wedding, I froze and for the next forty-five minutes I played over and over again, ad nauseam, "Oh Perfect Love." To this day when I hear that song I am twelve years old again, the groom has gone home to get the rings, and I am stuck on "Oh Perfect Love."

Little did I know that this was just the beginning!

Acknowledgments

There are many people who have encouraged me along the way in this endeavor. First, my sister-in-law, Daphne Scott, who made me realize I'd better start writing down the stories; the many customers who shared their stories and those who bared their souls and their personal insecurities in the course of shopping in T. Carolyn; my brother, the Rev. Dr. David Coolidge who served as a Minister of Music and Worship for over forty years, encouraged me with stories of his own, and helped initially with the editing; my wonderful daughter and excellent business partner, Terrie Tibbetts Martin, who has the most remarkable memory and helped me recall stories we had heard and kept her ears open for new stories in the course of our daily interacting with customers; Terrie's husband, my son-in-law, Dante Martin, founder of Global Marketing Solutions, who worked tirelessly on the design of the cover; my son Richard (who, incidentally, designed the T. Carolyn logo) and his wife, Tatiana Kober Tibbetts, president of Bejuba! Entertainment, both of whom first suggested that I expand the book to include advice that I give to my customers daily, suggested the title, and who gave me wonderful suggestions as I got closer to the end; and when my husband's and my eyes glazed over, a very dear and multi-talented member of our extended family, Jo Tibbetts, provided a pair of fresh eyes to proof read and make many valuable suggestions and corrections; and of course my husband, Owen, a product of the British educational system. Though an engineer by training, he is an excellent writer. Being retired, and with time on his hands, he and Jo devoted countless hours editing and refining my words to make the book stronger. With some difficulty I finally was able to convince him I was not attempting to create a literary masterpiece! In spite of it all he was always there to give moral support. In this venture we gained even more mutual respect.

Lastly, and to whom this book is dedicated, my late sister, Mary Beth Coolidge, J.D. She had been a professor of English Literature at Anderson University in Indiana for several years, then moved to Houston where she worked for Exxon Coal editing their newsletter, teaching writing courses and writing speeches for their executives. Taking advantage of Exxon's "golden handshake," she returned to law school at the prestigious South Texas College of Law in Houston and graduated with a law degree at the age of 45. She was my main source of encouragement in the beginning, and years later when she was diagnosed with multi-system atrophy (MSA) and could no longer continue her law practice or live alone, she moved in with my husband and me and continued to give suggestions and edit my manuscript right up until her death. Our mutual sense of humor kept us going through those difficult final two and a half years.

Mary, this is for you.

Introduction

As the daughter of missionaries, and having a degree in music, I have participated in many weddings of different cultures over the years. I thought I would be eminently qualified to help MOBs (mothers of the bride) and MOGs (mothers of the groom) in what I thought would be the relatively simple task of picking a dress to wear to their child's wedding.

Was I wrong! There's something about preparing for your child's wedding that brings out the best and the worst in some of us. I think hormones have a lot to do with this, and since most mothers are experiencing "hormonal surges," or as I like to call them "power surges," sometimes the most rational woman becomes the most irrational woman when it comes to picking out a dress to wear to her child's wedding.

Having served as a musician at many weddings in many different states and a foreign country, I had realized that much of the advice that was being given as "the gospel" was either incorrect or made no sense at all. Since the spring of 1991 when my daughter, Terrie, and I opened T. Carolyn, I have tried to help mothers find their way through a maze of misinformation to the only thing that really matters. I find myself exhorting mothers over and over again every day to "Look your best and show up!"

Because this dress is usually the second most photographed dress a mother will buy, her own wedding dress being *the* most photographed, mothers feel under extreme pressure to look their best. As fate would have it, most of us don't look the way we did when we were brides and this adds even more pressure. Added to this are the new "in-laws" and all the baggage that that carries! Because of all of the above, I have found that mothers confide in my daughter, sales staff and me far more than they would while purchasing any other garment.

The primary purpose of this book, therefore, is to answer questions common to all mothers of brides and grooms and to give valuable guidelines for selecting dresses for their children's weddings. I hope that this book will also prove to be entertaining.

Chapter 1

So, You've Just Been Told: You're Going to be the Mother of the Bride or the Mother of the Groom!

Fasten your seat belt! It's going to be a bumpy ride.

Suddenly, you begin to panic as you realize something has happened to your figure since you were a bride, and now you will be facing all those relatives and friends, and for some of you, your "exes." Some of these people you haven't seen in many years.

One mother emphatically told me, in the course of looking for a dress, that she couldn't understand why her son didn't get married four years earlier when she was fifty pounds lighter!

While you are thinking about how you look, your husband is, perhaps, quietly thinking about his wallet and the inevitable shrinkage that is about to take place. Ah, that the "shrinkage" could be your figure! This is usually the time when parents offer the couple money to elope!

It has been my experience that most mothers of the bride are so busy taking care of everyone else they generally put themselves last. Choosing what to wear to the wedding doesn't seem as high on her list of things to do as it is on the mother of the groom's list. The latter's focus is planning the rehearsal dinner and once this is taken care of, she's on to the "quest for her dress."

Traditionally, the mother of the bride (MOB) is the hostess of the wedding, and the mother of the groom

1

(MOG) is the most honored guest. You and she are **not** senior bridesmaids!

In a Christian wedding, your dress does not have to match or blend with the bridesmaids' dresses. Having said that let me hasten to add that the color of your dress should not *clash* with the bridesmaids' dresses either. And remember, I'm **not** talking about styles—I'm talking about **color.**

In a Jewish wedding, the parents will be standing close to the rabbi and in close proximity to the bridesmaids during the entire ceremony. The congregation will see them as part of a group. For this reason it's important that the mothers' and bridesmaids' dresses *blend*. Please note that I did **not** say that they have to match.

My definition of "clash" is a combination of colors that just don't go well together. Examples of colors that clash are red and orange, or orange and pink, as contrasted to blue and green, or brown and pink, which do not clash. I've been told by professional interior decorators that in decorating, blues, greens and browns are considered "neutrals," as they make up the background for everything in nature. Blue sky, green grass, brown earth and a myriad of colors make up the color pallet we are visually exposed to in nature every day. Everything goes with these three colors: blue, green and brown. Nothing clashes with them. Every flower has a green stem—no matter the color of the petals! We don't run around complaining that these things don't "match"! I had a mother once ask me if blue "really goes with green?" "If it doesn't," I replied, "You'd better speak to

God who made the bluebonnet (the state flower of Texas) with a green stem!"

When choosing your dress, it is extremely important that you *choose **your** very best color*, as this most likely will be your most photographed event, aside from your own wedding.

I've heard a thousand times, "I don't want to mess up the pictures." Most brides and mothers are not aware that parents are not usually photographed with the wedding party. They are photographed with the bride and groom, and, of course, there is usually a family picture. It is important to realize that the family picture is *not* the basis on which you choose your dress. At the risk of sounding redundant, I will say it again and again throughout this book: ***Choose the dress you look best in! Don't settle for anything less.*** Please notice that I said, "Choose the dress **you** look best in." I did **not** say, "Choose the most expensive dress you can afford!" There's a **big** difference, as this book will explain.

Once the bride has chosen the bridesmaids' dresses, as the mother of the bride, you can begin choosing what you will wear. If the bride has chosen floor length gowns for the bridesmaids, you can choose any length you wish. Remember, however, that a floor length gown will make you look taller and slimmer, two adjectives that seem to be very important to most mothers!

If one mother decides to wear long, the other mother should wear long. Generally the mother of the bride makes this decision. This is for balance and symmetry in the "bookend" picture, as I call it. In this picture, the bride and groom are in the middle; the parents are on either side. If one mother wears a short dress, she will be the only one in that picture with her legs showing. She will not appear to be as "formal" as the others.

If one mother wears a pantsuit, and there are occasions when this has been the choice, the other mother should wear a long dress or a pantsuit. This way both women have their legs covered in the pictures.

Traditionally, mothers were advised to wear short dresses if the bridesmaids' dresses were short. I no longer believe that this is necessary. I have seen many instances that have reinforced this belief. As long as the bride is wearing a long gown and the men are wearing tuxedos, mothers should feel free to wear a long dress if that is their choice. Again, remember that long dresses tend to make one appear taller and slimmer.

Although this book is not about men's wear, a brief discussion of men's formal wear is necessary. It dictates the degree of formality of the wedding and what the women should wear. Decades ago, tuxedos (also called black tie attire) were considered appropriate only for evening wear. Nowadays, this is no longer the case. If the groom and groomsmen are wearing tuxedos, the mothers should wear fancy short or long dresses. Both are acceptable with black tie attire. Certainly, for an evening wedding the mothers' dresses should be long, as a long dress provides a more formal look. Obviously, if it is an ultra-formal white tie wedding, the mothers' dresses should be long. Once the bride and groom have researched appropriate dress codes and have decided for themselves the degree of formality for their wedding, the mothers can then proceed to select their dresses knowing whether the wedding is to be ultra-formal, formal, semi-formal, dressy casual, or casual.

Mothers have asked me if you can really have a formal wedding before six in the evening. The answer is, "Yes." Weddings can be formal regardless of the time of day. After all, Charles and Diana's wedding was in the morning—you can't get much more formal than that! There are over 60,000 weddings in Houston every year. There are only fifty-two Saturdays and fifty-two Sundays. Go figure! Not everyone can have a seven o'clock wedding.

I've had women tell me that they'd like to wear a "church" dress to their child's wedding. I then ask them whether the men in the wedding party will be wearing tuxedos. If they say, "Yes." I then say, "I'll go along with that as long as you see men wearing tuxes to church on Sundays!" If the men in the wedding party are wearing tuxedos, the wedding is sufficiently formal that the mothers should wear a formal dress or gown.

Often with disastrous results, many mothers feel it necessary to allow the bride to choose what they will wear. Brides are *only* responsible for dressing *brides-maids*. **Mothers should dress themselves!**

Obviously, you can certainly include the bride in your decision-making; but be careful or you may end up wearing something you really don't like and in which you don't feel good. When one has a less than perfect figure, choosing your own dress is a very personal thing.

I've watched Size 4 brides pick out Size 4 styles for mothers who are Size 18 and above. Choose your own dress! Let's face it; you've been dressing yourself quite successfully for a number of years. If you don't feel that you can trust your own judgment, put yourself in the hands of an honest, professional, reputable sales staff that is in the business of making you look your best.

I always advise a bride that the best "gift" she can give her mother and her future mother-in-law is to encourage each to pick something that makes her feel beautiful and something that will photograph well.

It is important to understand that both mothers have their own individual sense of style. One may be an accountant, the other an artist. They do *not* lose their individuality. Each brings to this occasion her personal sense of style. Mothers are *not* "senior bridesmaids" who have to "match." Remember, the only thing that has to match is length. If one mother wears long, the other wears long; if one mother wears short, the other wears short. *The mother of the bride traditionally chooses the length of the dress that she and the mother of the groom will wear.*

Mothers are in the "hostess" and "most honored guest" category and, therefore, better dressed than the other guests. As stated earlier, the mother of the bride is traditionally the hostess and the mother of the groom the most honored guest. At all times you, the mother, will be surrounded by a sea of color called "guests"—people who have gone to their closets that day and chosen to wear what they look best in. *For goodness sake, mothers should do the same!*

In trying to get to know each of my customers better, I always ask, "What did you envision wearing to this occasion?"

A lady who was a Size 18 or 20 remarked, "First, I envisioned being a Size 4!"

"I envisioned an elopement!" If I've heard this once I've heard it a hundred times!

"Anything but 'matronly'."

In eighteen years, I haven't had one mother tell me she wants to look like a "mother." Neither have I had one tell me she wants to look older or heavier! These are things we take for granted. It is interesting though, what some perceive to be "matronly." Sometimes, I will pick out a style in a particular color for a customer and be thrilled at how good she looks, only to be told she feels "matronly." She then proceeds to pick out a dress I had to force myself to select for the store because *I* thought it was "matronly," and she is thrilled.

I have come to realize that "matronly" is a very personal frame of reference, influenced by someone in the customer's past—an aunt, a schoolteacher, etc. To advise properly, I have to listen to the customer and find out what she considers "matronly." Sometimes the customer will begin to describe the dress she thinks she is looking for, and she will describe the most matronly dress imaginable—at least in *my* frame of reference!

I strongly suggest that, on your first outing, you go alone. I know this is contrary to what most people will advise, but this will give you a chance to see what choices are available and you can begin to form your *own* opinion as to what you would like to wear. After you have narrowed down your choices, you may wish to bring with you the bride, your husband, or your best friend. Remember, though, the more people you bring, the more opinions you are going to get, solicited or not. This will make it more difficult for you to make a decision without hurting someone's feelings.

Believe it or not, I have actually seen "friends" unwittingly booby-trap friends, or perhaps even sabotage "friends." I have seen women put something on and be transformed, whereupon the friend remarks, "It doesn't look like you. Take it off!" It may not be how she normally looks, but this is how she *should* look!

Mothers of the groom often feel it is their duty to "check" with the bride when deciding on a dress. Unfortunately, this often opens a can of worms. You could be losing control over what you will be wearing. If you have found something you absolutely adore—the dress of your dreams—and the bride decides, for whatever reason, that she prefers something else, you will now be forced to make a choice. You can give up the dress of your dreams or go against her wishes! Neither will bode well. Just don't do it!

One afternoon a very quiet, demure lady came into the store and pulled me aside. Almost in a whisper, she informed me that she was going to be the mother of the groom and the wedding was going to be in New Jersey. Oh yes, and she really needed to look good.

I took her by the arm and began quietly to reassure her that we would be able to help her look her best. She was a "winter," I mentioned, and her best colors were the stronger, more vibrant cool colors.

"But the bride told me that those colors won't go with the wedding!" she exclaimed.

About that time a blonde bombshell rounded the corner and proclaimed that she was the bride and that she'd flown in from New Jersey to dress her mother-in-law-to-be.

I responded, a bit tongue in cheek, that this was a novel concept since I was sure this dear lady had been dressing herself for a good many years and was quite capable of continuing to do so, even for this occasion.

Undaunted, the bride brushed my comment aside and repeated that she had flown all the way to Houston to pick out the dress for her mother-in-law.

I explained, as I always do, that for this lady to look her best and to photograph her best she needed to wear one of her good colors.

"But that won't go with the wedding! Everything in the wedding is soft and pastel."

"Have you asked *all* your guests to wear pastels?" I questioned.

"Of course not," she replied.

"Then since your future mother-in-law is sitting two rows up from the congregation of people who went to their closets and picked out what they look best in, we should not deprive this lady of the same privilege." I went on to explain that, after all, she would be mingling with these guests at the reception and there would be no bonus points for blending and matching with bridesmaids and flowers if she didn't look her best.

At this point the groom rounded the corner. He had overheard the exchange.

"I know you own the shop and all that," he interjected, "but this is my bride-to-be and you are arguing with her."

"I would like to think I'm raising her consciousness level, and besides, all I'm concerned with is helping your mother to look her best, something that I would think you, of all people, would appreciate."

The price of honesty is sometimes no sale. It was obvious I could not help these people, so I drifted off to help others. About twenty minutes later they left the store empty-handed.

I never saw them again, but I'm sure my advice came back to haunt them when they saw their wedding pictures.

Once you've found that special dress, I recommend strongly that you inform the bride that the dress you've chosen makes you feel beautiful and will photograph well. What bride is going to challenge that? (Well, in all honesty, I have come in contact with some who have challenged the choice. I cover this in an upcoming chapter.)

And last, but not least, be prepared for friction between you and your child. No matter how close you two have been, you are likely going to experience times when you become so exasperated that you want to clobber her and times when you don't even recognize her because of her behavior.

When our children were in their teenage years, my husband and I attended a series of lectures by John Bradshaw who has become an extremely well known and internationally recognized counselor, lecturer and author.

About 200 of us crowded into the room to attend the lecture series, "Adolescence and Mid-Life Crisis."

I took away from those lectures many helpful and interesting things, but perhaps the most important was what John referred to as "distancing." He explained that leaving the "nest," whether it is going off to college or getting married, is so scary your child has to make you out to be the "bad guy," so that leaving isn't so painful. If everything is "hunky dory," your child will not have the courage to leave home.

Remember this when, suddenly, there are more arguments or criticism from your once oh-so-close child. Tell yourself not to take it personally. Your child is just *"distancing,"* a process, according to Bradshaw, which is very normal and necessary.

Chapter 2

The Wedding is WHEN?

One Saturday afternoon, about 1:30, a woman who appeared to be a Size 24W, came through the door clutching a shoebox to her breast. I have learned not to ask, "Are you the mother at a wedding?" If the lady happens to be a *bride* for the fourth time she will be incensed that I would think she is the *mother* of the bride. Instead, I ask, "Do you have a special occasion coming up?" This lady indicated that she was the mother of the bride. I congratulated her and asked when the wedding was to take place. Still clutching her shoebox, she replied, "Tonight at 6 o'clock." I tried to keep calm and not hyperventilate. I asked her what she thought she would like to wear. She opened her shoebox and produced a pair of lilac/pink leather shoes with a pair of pantyhose squashed on top. "Something to go with these," was her reply. A favorite saying of a good friend of mine, who was a criminal defense attorney, flashed through my mind, "And the people in hell want ice water too!" My mind raced, but I tried to remain calm as I began to search through the many dresses we had on hand. Miraculously, we had the perfect dress and, almost as miraculously, no alterations were necessary.

Curiosity is one of my obvious traits. Wondering how in the world she could find herself four and a half hours away from her daughter's wedding without a dress was driving me crazy. I imagined there was a juicy story here. Perhaps some calamity had happened to her dress at the last minute—as had happened when a woman called us from Galveston in a panic because her grandson had spilled red Kool-Aid on her dress the night before the wedding. "So, what happened to your dress?" "What dress?" was her reply. "Your dress for the wedding!" I said. "Oh, I never had one," she said. "I hadn't been feeling too well and I wasn't too sure I'd be able to go. But I feel fine now, so I'm going." She calmly sat down, helped herself to the refreshments we always have in the store, drank a cup of coffee and left with her purchase on her way to the hairdresser's.

After she left, I went to the back of the store and told my daughter about this. "Mom, there's got to be another story to this. There's probably a husband or an ex-husband who is or isn't showing up. That's what probably made her decide to go." I was relating this to someone else a few days later, and I think she probably hit the nail on the head when she replied, "She's probably finally speaking to the bride!"

Very few of our customers are this nonchalant about their child's wedding, yet many put themselves under additional stress because of unnecessary procrastination. Indecision breeds procrastination. The pattern often goes something like this:

Months before the wedding, a woman comes in and narrows her selection down to four dresses. She leaves with the assertion that she'll be back. (We often refer to these as "be-backs.") Sure enough, six weeks later she comes back, this time with a friend who is an "expert," known in the industry as the KIAF, the "Know-It-All-Friend." This friend or relative has come to give her advice and to help her decide. By now, two of the dresses are gone and are either no longer available, or cannot be delivered before the wedding. One of these happens to be her favorite, even though she couldn't make up her mind to buy it the first time. A month later, the scene is repeated and, by now, only one of the four, her least favorite, remains. She still can't decide. Two weeks before the wedding she comes back, and the fourth dress is gone.

By her indecision, she has put herself under months of stress that could have been avoided. As a consequence, she has to start the process all over again. She must purchase something off the rack that day or risk not having time for necessary alterations. She has, in fact, let others—those who purchased the four dresses she initially selected—make the decision for her.

Every day we have mothers who come into the store and think that every dress we have can be reordered and is available in all colors. Having recently left the bridal salon, where the bridal gowns and bridesmaids' dresses may be available on order for up to two years in most designs, they assume that the same is true of mothers' dresses. Nothing could be further from the truth!

Many of the less expensive dresses, the ones often found in department stores, are mass-produced in large quantities, but seldom re-cut. However, this applies not only to department store dresses. Many of the higher priced dresses are restricted to a relatively small number of units before the manufacturing of that design is discontinued, thereby also rendering them impossible to be reordered. The reason for this is covered in more detail in Chapter 10.

One Saturday morning, my daughter encountered a lady dressed in a sweatshirt and jeans, and no make-up. She said that her son was getting married that evening.

As she was working her way through the racks of Size 8 dresses, she mused out loud that she really needed to stop procrastinating, because she had sold her home, the new owners would be moving into it in four days, and all her belongings were in boxes. She still had no idea where she was going to move to, and now her son was getting married in five hours and she still hadn't bought a dress! Because we take our customers' needs very seriously, these situations cause us great stress. It is times like these I'm reminded of the well-known maxim, "Failure to plan on your part does not constitute an emergency on my part!"

One customer, who hailed from a small East Texas town, related an earlier experience when another of her children was getting married. She had taken her dress in to the local dry cleaner to have it pressed for the wedding. Being somewhat of a procrastinator, she put off picking it up until the day of the wedding. To her horror, she discovered that the dry cleaner was always closed on Saturdays! She frantically tried to find out who the owner was so that she could beseech him to open up and let her get her dress for the wedding. As she worked for the local taxing authority, she even tried tracking down the owner through the tax records, but to no avail. Finally she began calling all the other cleaners in the town asking if they, by chance, knew the owner. Luckily, one of the other cleaners was able to give her that information. She then was able to contact the owner who willingly retrieved her dress. She swore she would never procrastinate again!

It continues to intrigue me that mothers of the bride, and mothers in general, tend to put themselves last. In actuality, I guess this is what makes a mom a "good mom." We tend to take care of everyone else in the family first, and, in the case of a wedding, the mother of the bride, especially, is so busy taking care of everyone else and helping to plan the wedding that her "needs" are shoved to the back burner. As a result, the "last minute mom" is someone I continue to see frequently.

One Friday afternoon, the phone rang and the lady on the other end asked if we carried dresses in Size 16. I explained that we carried all sizes, Sizes 2 petite to 32 women's. I asked her when her special occasion was, and she told me that it was the next day. She went on to explain that there was a reason she was running late. She was making the bride's gown and she "was a little late with the pearls." She wanted something in red. Two hours later she appeared in the store. Again, God was with us and we found the perfect suit. Her husband was happy, the bride was happy, and she was happy. (Terrie and I were hyperventilating, as she had no idea how lucky she was, due to the color she wanted and the figure problems she presented.)

How did she let this go until the day before the wedding? She explained to us that she was at the church spraying some of the altar decorations for the wedding, when one of the altar committee ladies asked her what she planned to wear to the wedding the next day. When she indicated that she hadn't found her dress yet, the lady urged her to go to T. Carolyn because she had known another lady who had found something there at the last minute! Flattered as I was at the recommendation, it worried me that we would become a haven for procrastinating moms and add further to our stress level!

After she left, Terrie and I were discussing the situation and I explained to her that the lady had been making the bride's gown and was behind on sewing on the pearls. Terrie commented that she could not understand anyone making a bridal gown in this day and age with so many relatively inexpensive gowns being readily available. I explained, in my great wisdom, that I was sure it was because of the sentiment involved. "Sentiment?" snorted Terrie, "Sentiment is not being glued to a sewing machine for four months and sewing on pearls hours before the wedding! Sentiment is going shopping, deciding on a wedding gown and doing lunch afterwards!" So much for the younger generation's view of "sentiment"!

Perhaps the ultimate in procrastination is the story told to us by a former employee whose husband frequently sang at weddings. At one wedding where he was the soloist, the start was delayed by 2½ hours because the mother of the bride was still out shopping for a dress! Needless to say, this caused a great deal of hostility between her and the bride and the groom.

Over the years I've heard various reasons and rationalizations why the customer is out looking for a dress at the last minute:

"I wasn't sure the wedding was going to actually take place!"

"We recently moved to the city, and the movers packed the box with my dress in it with the items going into storage. We haven't a clue which box it is in."

"The mother of the bride has changed her mind and has decided at the last minute to wear a long gown. My dress is short!"

"My grandson spilled red Kool-Aid on my dress and the wedding is tomorrow!"

"I haven't had time. I've been too busy taking care of everyone else."

"The store where I bought my dress and where it was being altered say they've lost it."

"I had my dress made, and today, when I tried it on, I looked like a stuffed sausage!"

"The alterations lady ruined both my dress and my mother's."

"I was having something made and now that it's finished, I don't like it!" (If I had a dollar for every time I'd heard this one, I could retire.)

"I ordered something on the Internet and now I'm told the shipping company has lost it!" (Hmmm...no tracking number, huh? I don't think it was actually shipped.)

"The airline lost my luggage!"

"I ordered it on the Internet and they didn't send the size I ordered. I can't get them to return my calls and the 5-day grace period is up."

"I thought I was going to lose some weight!"

"I was put on a new medication and I've put on so much weight I can't wear my dress!"

And conversely, "I've been ill and have lost so much weight the alterations lady says it can't possibly be made to fit!"

"You won't believe it, but I've just found out the other mother has the exact same dress I chose."

"The mother of the bride has *five* things hanging in her closet and she just told me that she'll decide the *morning* of the wedding which one she will wear! They range from a short cocktail suit to a fully beaded gown! I already have a full-length gown. Now I need a short dress as well!"

Sometimes, it really *is* no one's fault.

One young lady came into the store looking for something in ivory that looked "sort of 'bridal-ish' but not too 'bridal-ish.' " She went on to say that she and her husband were having a reception to celebrate their marriage, which had taken place nine months before. She added that she *had* planned her wedding—but in *just four hours*!

The groom was a lieutenant in the reserves and was given notice on a Tuesday that he was being assigned to the United Nations Peace-keeping Mission in Bosnia and would be leaving the country on Saturday. The bride hurriedly called her mom, who was in the midst of last minute arrangements for a block party, and asked her to call a judge who was a family friend. Meanwhile, the bride and groom rushed down to the courthouse to obtain their marriage license. Because he was a member of the armed services, there was no mandatory waiting period.

At the block party, the mother of the bride informed the neighbors, as they arrived, that there was going to be a wedding. Since everyone was dressed in shorts and jeans, the bride opted to wear shorts also. The bride's grandmother picked up a generic cake at the grocery store on the way, and the bride's aunt's cake topper was placed strategically on the "wedding cake." The bride's grandparents' 50th wedding anniversary wine goblets were brought out. With the judge officiating, the wedding proceeded much to the delight of the surprised guests.

The honeymoon? Since the groom was supposed to be in San Antonio the next day to begin processing for Bosnia, the couple left immediately for the four-hour drive to San Antonio. Wednesday was spent with the groom taking care of his military obligations on base. And—oh yes—the bride had to prepare to leave for Austin that evening. She had recently graduated from chiropractic school and was scheduled to take her state board exams on Thursday. Saturday, the groom left for Bosnia. Fortunately, they were able to meet in Europe later for a belated honeymoon. When I met the bride, he had been gone nine months and was due home in two weeks, hence the need for a nice dress for the reception.

While helping a mother one morning, she began to tell me the most incredible story I think I've ever heard. Around 5 a.m., the day of her wedding, Neiman-Marcus in Dallas burned to the ground. This happened in 1964. It was a ten million dollar loss—the costliest department store fire in U.S. history up to that point in time. The tradition of the day was for Neiman's to keep the bridal gowns and deliver them to the church on the day of the wedding. "At 8 o'clock that same morning, while having my hair done," our customer related, "I overheard another patron talking about the fire. My hairdresser commented that I should be glad I didn't have my gown at Neiman's. Suddenly, with a jolt, I realized that *my* gown *was* at Neiman's—and my wedding was to take place at 4 o'clock that afternoon! Another patron in the salon kindly offered to let me have her nail appointment so that I could leave sooner. Because my mother suffered from anxiety, I felt that I needed to tell her about the fire in person, rather than by phone. Meanwhile, my mother had received a call from a Neiman's representative telling her of the catastrophe. They assured her that one way or the other they would find another gown for her daughter.

My mother, not wanting to alarm me, decided to wait until I got home to tell me what had happened.

"Just as I reached home, Neiman's called again and asked that I come to a nearby hotel where they would have several bridal gowns that they had acquired and would have alterations people standing by to take care of anything that needed to be done. It was only then that my mother and I found out that each of us already knew about the fire."

Apparently, there were 10 weddings to be held that day that involved bridal gowns from Neiman's, but because our customer's wedding was the first one, she had top priority. When she arrived at the hotel, true to their word, four seamstresses and twenty gowns were awaiting her. (Neiman's had hurriedly flown in gowns from their Houston store.) Because she was a Size 2, the sample Size 8 gowns where huge on her, but the seamstresses began frantically pinning the dress and taking in vast amounts of fabric. Shortly thereafter, the seamstresses left the hotel, the chosen gown in tow, and headed back to their shop. In mid afternoon, the bride and her parents made their way to the church. At ten minutes to four, the finished gown arrived and fit like a glove! And the wedding went off without a hitch.

Such commitment to service is remarkable and all too rare. One wonders how many stores today would provide this kind of service. Yet, commitment to this level of service to the customer should be the goal of every business, regardless of size. The mother who was relating this story to me had brought a friend along to help her choose her MOB dress. When the story was finished, the friend turned to me and said, "They've been married 44 years, so obviously it wasn't a sign of bad luck!"

While we have seen many customers who procrastinate, we have also had customers who have made quick decisions.

One day, about a year after we opened the store, a customer came in to buy a dress for her child's wedding that was five months away. We picked out three dresses that we knew she would look best in and in twenty minutes she had decided on the one that she wanted. Since this was the first customer to make such a quick decision, we were curious and asked her a few things about herself. It turned out that she was a nurse in the neo-natal intensive care unit in a major hospital in the enormous and world-famous Houston Medical Center.

The next to make a quick decision was a nurse on the Houston Life Flight helicopters that provide emergency air ambulance service for the critically ill or injured. She was followed by a counselor on the Suicide Crisis Hotline. These women all made moment-to-moment decisions which could mean life or death for someone. Other decisive customers have been business owners, judges, financial advisors and high-level managers in large corporations and some stay-at-home mothers. But let's face it, not all career women are decisive. In almost all careers and all walks of life there are indecisive people.

It is amazing the number of women who, unable to bring themselves to make a decision, use the rationale, "Oh well, if it is meant to be my dress it will be here when I return." The implication is that somehow it is left to God or fate. Such people would do well to remember the old adage, "God helps those who help themselves"! Many customers think that because a particular dress is available in the store today it will be there six weeks or two months from now. This could *not* be further from the truth. Why do we not emphasize this more strongly to our customers? Because we do not want any customer to think that we are pressuring them into making a premature decision. We have had indecisive customers come back to the store two months later (sometimes two *hours* later!) and exclaim, almost in an accusatory tone, "You've sold my dress!" They're distressed to find out that the dress is gone and cannot be reordered. They're crushed and are forced to start their search all over again. Terrie has often said to me, "Mom, I'd like to tell some of these women, 'If it were *your* dress it would be in *your* closet!' and I would like to remind others that that's what we do here: we sell dresses, we're not a museum!"

When dresses can be ordered, customers are sometimes surprised at how long it *might* take. If the dress you want has to be ordered, and it's not in the manufacturer's inventory here in this country but, instead, has to be ordered from the factory (usually overseas), delivery can take **12 weeks or longer.** Remember, dresses are never manufactured as one of a kind—they're made as one of many during a planned production run. So when a dress has to be ordered, 12 weeks really is *not* a lot of time when you think of what's involved: ordering, manufacturing, shipping to the United States, clearance through U.S. Customs and shipping from the vendor to the store where you are purchasing your dress.

Every day I'm asked, "When should I begin looking for my dress?" This depends on your comfort zone. Some women are content if their dress arrives the day before the wedding. Others are frantic if it isn't hanging in their closet a month before the wedding. Everyone has her own comfort level. Obviously, the sooner you begin looking, the sooner you'll begin to get an idea of what your options are.

My recommendation is to begin your search **at least** *five but preferably six months* before the wedding is to take place. This will give you enough time to find a dress, enough time to order it, (if ordering is necessary) and enough time for delivery and alterations. During the Chinese New Year, which falls between January 20th and February 19th, depending on the lunar calendar, factories in China will be shutdown for about a month. Since most mother's dresses and bridal gowns are now made in China, this can result in an increase of four weeks to the delivery time for dresses manufactured around this time of the year.

Suffice is to say if you try on a dress that you really like and it fits your body and your budget, you would be well advised to consider buying it. If you don't, there is a very good chance that it will not be available the next time you visit the store. Ask yourself, "How will I feel if I can no longer buy this dress?" This may help you to make a decision.

If you can't trust your own judgment, find a store that you can trust—a store with a staff who is genuinely interested in what's best for you, and who will give you honest, accurate and helpful advice. Finding such a store is covered in more detail in Chapters 10 and 12.

With the selection of your dress behind you, you can turn your attention to other details about the wedding without your own dress becoming a bigger problem by the week.

Chapter 3

So, You're Going To Lose Weight?

Ninety-nine percent of the mothers I see indicate they are going to go on a diet—that four-letter word that conjures up all sorts of false images. Most women don't realize that it takes a loss of as much as *15 pounds* to equal *one* dress size–particularly in the larger size dresses.

Planning to lose weight is the number one reason women procrastinate in purchasing a dress. They put off even trying on a dress because they are on a diet, or are going to go on a diet. They've set this weight goal. As a result, I've seen women, all too often, come into the store refusing to get serious about choosing a dress. They have decided to wait until they reach their goal before exploring their options. I will often see these customers every two weeks, and they are getting *bigger and bigger,* instead of smaller and smaller! The stress of planning the wedding and the indecision about the dress are actually causing them to *put on weight* rather than lose it, in spite of the diet!

I always encourage these ladies to find a dress and relax. I have actually found that, once the stress of finding a dress has been eliminated, the customer is much more successful in losing weight. If the weight comes off, as it often does in these circumstances, the side seams can always be taken in.

For years I have encouraged women to relax, eat healthfully and exercise. But what if the weight doesn't come off? Here's what it all comes down to: let's find a dress that *looks* as though you've been on a diet. Often, this is actually easier than trying to lose weight while experiencing the added stress of an up-coming wedding.

When you've worked with as many women as we have, for as many years as we have, you recognize the styles, colors, and fabrics, that will create the "miracle" dress. These are the dresses that will make a woman appear to be two dress sizes smaller, *and these styles do exist in all price ranges.*

Terrie was working with a customer one day. Even though the sides of the zipper were about four inches apart, the lady exclaimed, "Five more pounds and I'll have it!"

One customer asked, if she lost 15 pounds before the wedding, could she bring the dress back and exchange it for a smaller size. She went on to explain that the wedding was in ten days! Short of a miracle medical breakthrough or a horrible disease, we couldn't see this happening!

I remember vividly the lovely lady who went to one of the weight loss centers that promote rapid weight loss. She did, indeed, lose the weight, but the week before the wedding, she had to buy a wig because her hair was falling out!

Terrie has often said to me, "Mom, I'd love to tell the customers we don't sell 'miracle dresses' that make you look twenty-five years younger, fifty pounds lighter, and make the new wife with the plastic surgery disappear!" We do the best we can, but sometimes the situation is so sticky nothing can make the customer happy. This is always difficult for us to accept, but we've learned not to take it personally.

With the advent of undergarments like Spanx, many women have found they can slip into a smaller size dress. Particularly helpful is the Higher Power panty girdle by Spanx, which fits just below the bra and down to the lower thigh, helping to smooth out "love handles" and create a leaner look in the tummy and midriff area. The fact that there are no side seams in this garment helps to create a smooth profile and enables the wearer to look thinner and sleeker. Designed by a woman, most customers remark at how comfortable this panty girdle is to wear.

Often our son-in-law, Dante, will come to the store on a very busy Saturday and man the cash register so that all of us women can help customers try on and select dresses. Frequently, this means he has to forgo a golf game to help us out.

One Saturday, a customer brought her dress to the cash register, noticed the Spanx display nearby and said to Dante, "I wonder if these Spanx really work?" "Sure they do," was his reply, "they actually will help you look slimmer." "How would *you* know? Have *you* ever tried them on?" she challenged. "Actually, I *have* tried a pair on. I figured if I were going to sell these things, I'd better know what they do and how they feel." With that she grabbed a pair off the rack and said, "O.K. I'll take a pair!"

Another time he was encouraging a customer to try on a pair of Spanx. "Just try them on over your underwear and you'll see how great they are." "But I'm not wearing any underwear," she volunteered. Evidently the visual that flashed through his mind was so vivid that he blurted out with a laugh, "I think it's time for me to go back to the golf course!"

Chapter 4

Does Size REALLY Matter?

Obviously, for health reasons it does, and lets face it, 99.9 percent of all women obsess about their weight. I haven't had *one* woman in eighteen years give the impression that she was happy with her body or her appearance. This even includes the pageant girls we worked with for a period of time!

My husband, a naturalized American, who has traveled in many parts of the world for business and pleasure, declares that, without a doubt, American women are the best looking women in the world. He contends that they make more of an effort to enhance what God has given them than any other group of women he has seen.

An English friend, who had been our neighbor when we lived in Trinidad, came to Houston on a business trip several years ago. It was his first trip to America. After we had spent a day of sight-seeing and were having a lovely dinner, he remarked to me that, when he returned home to England, he would have to tell his teenage son that all the women in Texas did, indeed, look like the women in the television show "Dallas."

And yet, my husband contends American Caucasian women seem to have the worst self-esteem. He attributes this to the fact that, throughout their lives, they are continuously being bombarded with magazine, newspaper, television and radio advertisements where they are told they don't measure up–they don't smell as good as they could, they don't look as good as they should, their complexion isn't quite right, their hair isn't quite right, their makeup isn't quite right, even their nails aren't quite right and, in fact, nothing is quite right about them.

This also reminds me of the time this little Size 8 older lady came in to select a dress for her 50th wedding anniversary. She was really quite tiny and petite but had just a little bit of a tummy. When she finally decided which dress she liked best she placed a call to her husband who was on the golf course.

A short time later he arrived. He was generally overweight and had quite a "beer belly" that hung over his belt. I took him to where his wife was awaiting his approval of the dress she had chosen. "Isn't it marvelous that, after all these years, she is still so small?" I asked him. "Well, she was even smaller when I married her!" he halfway snorted. I wasn't about to let him get away with that, so I quickly replied while casting my eye towards the amplest portion of his anatomy, "I imagine you were too!"

Terrie briefly looked at me in disbelief and fled to the back office. Quickly closing the door behind her, she burst out laughing, and said to her father, " Dad, you'll never believe what Mom just told a customer!" After I had admonished the husband, there was this moment of suspenseful silence. He then burst into laughter, approved the dress and left a happy customer.

One of my favorite sayings is, "Life is not a dress rehearsal." In other words: this is it! When I was in college, I was a Size 7. I considered myself to be big then. I tell customers, "God only knew how big I could get!" I would give anything to be a "big" Size 7 now! I wasted all those years yearning to be even smaller and now see where I am! Oh, well, I've learned my lesson.

I advise women all day long to accept the size they are and *learn to dress it*. Don't go through life miserable about the pounds on your bones while not getting any smaller. So many women have their self-esteem tied to their weight! Obviously, if you are at an unhealthy weight you should try to do something about it. But, for heaven's sake, don't waste each day obsessing about your weight. If you do, you will miss out on many of the wonderful things and experiences life has to offer.

Shortly after Margaret had come to work for us (we stole her from a maternity shop when Terrie was pregnant with her first child) she came to the back office where I was working on the computer.

"Barbara," she said, "There's a woman out there threatening to kill herself!"

"Not in MY store!" I muttered under my breath as I quickly made my way onto the sales floor.

There, seated in a chair, was a large lady, Size 26W, with tears rolling down her cheeks. Her brother was getting married and she wasn't happy with the way she looked and didn't want to attend the wedding.

I explained to her that she was like a snowflake. No one else in the entire world was exactly like her. God intended for her to be unique. What she needed to do was to find something in a wonderful color, fix her hair and makeup, hold her head up high and "waltz" right into the wedding.

As the customer left an hour later, her purchase slung over her arm, I turned to Margaret and asked, "Did you ever have *this* happen in the maternity shop?!" "Heavens, no!" Margaret replied.

Neither I nor the sales rep will ever forget the day he came to show me the silicone, stick-on bras for the "women who wanted to be larger." (These are silicone, sticky cups that fasten in the middle and literally stick onto your breasts. They adhere to your body in such a way that you don't need to wear a bra, they will actually give you a bust "lift" and, even while wearing a light colored or shear fabric, your nipples will not be exposed.) After having been given the sales pitch on the merits of this item, I asked Terrie to come to the back office.

"Hey, Terrie! Look what Eddie has brought for us to see. These are for women who want larger busts," I said. "Where are your crotch enhancers, Eddie? I think we women will need bust enhancers when you guys need crotch enhancers!" was her reply. Having worked with so many small-busted women who are made to feel inadequate, Terrie is particularly sensitive to this issue.

To this day, whenever I see Eddie at market or on a road visit, he still reminds me of that incident!

Until my husband's hearing became a severe problem, he would occasionally come to the store on Saturdays and help out by answering the phone in the back office. Owen is extremely good at giving directions as most engineers are, and it was a way he could help and, thereby, let me spend more time on the sales floor.

Following one of the calls, he came to me on the floor quite concerned and explained he had just spoken with a woman who had a big problem.

"What's the problem?" I asked. "Well," Owen began haltingly, "she says she has a really big problem. Her breasts are very large. She went on and on about the size of her bust and what a problem it was. I could hardly get her off of the phone. She seemed desperate to find someone who could help her. So, I told her I was sure you could, as you've helped many women with all sorts of figure problems. I asked her to tell me what she would be wearing so that you'll be able to recognize her and help her personally. She said that wasn't necessary because you'll realize she's here the moment she walks through the door. I asked her to tell me anyway, so she said she'd be wearing a black sweater to disguise the size of her large bust. So, just be on the lookout for a woman with a very large bust wearing a black sweater. She really needs help, and I promised her that you, personally, would help her." Sure enough, an hour or so later she showed up.

Later that evening, as we were driving home, Owen brought up the subject of the woman with the "big problem." "You know," he said, "that lady didn't have *that* large a bust. She was just large all over!" Clearly, he had been thinking about this for a while. "Barbara," he then continued seriously, "I think that woman was actually getting a thrill out of talking to me about her big breasts. When I agreed to help at T. Carolyn no one told me that I would have to contend with *phone sex!*" he exclaimed. I laughed so hard I nearly ran off the road!

Most women are not aware that there can be as much as two and a half inches difference in a given size between different manufacturers. This is why I always advise customers to look up or down one or *two* sizes when selecting things to try on. You just absolutely **cannot** go by the size label! I have come to the conclusion that there is more standardization in women's shoe sizes than there is in women's clothing sizes.

I've frequently had customers refuse, somewhat indignantly, to try on a particular size that they really needed. "I'm not trying on a Size 18!!" The size label is just made up of little numbers that no one sees when you're wearing the dress. A garment that is snug in any area of the body will make a woman look larger than she actually is. A woman who says she is a Size 16, for example, will often adamantly refuse to try on a dress labeled Size 18. We then have to ask, "*Whose* Size 16 are you?" One manufacturer's sizes may run large; another manufacturer's sizes may run small; still another manufacturer's sizes will run somewhere in between. Thus, one manufacturer's Size 16 may correspond to another manufacturer's Size 18 or to yet another manufacturer's Size 14!

I re-emphasize, **don't** get hung up on the numbers! We can guarantee you that no one at the wedding is going to walk up to you and unzip your dress and look at the size label inside to see what size you're wearing! Size numbers are **not** important! The way the garment fits you and the right color are the two most important factors in choosing your dress.

There are actually four size *categories* that women have to choose from. These categories are:

- Missy (also known as "Standard")
     Garments in this size range are typically offered in Sizes 4–18 and sometimes 20.

- Petite (P)
     Garments in this size range are typically offered in Sizes 2P–18P
     Note: Sizes 2P, 16P and 18P are often hard to find.

- Women's Petite (WP)
     Garments in this size range are typically offered in Sizes 14WP–28WP

- Women's (W)
     Garments in this size range are typically offered in Sizes 14W–28W

If a woman is short-waisted she should choose either a "Petite" or a "Women's Petite," depending on her bust, waist and hip measurements. If she is long-waisted, she should choose either a "missy" or "women's." Obviously, in all cases skirts may have to be hemmed, depending on the height of the individual.

The following tables give an *indication* of the size differences in garments when going from one size to another. They do **not** represent any particular manufacturer's sizing measurements. Each manufacturer will have their own measurements for each of their sizes, so size *differences* can vary from one manufacturer to the next as can the *actual* bust, waist and hip measurements for any given size–further proof that *the size marked on the label doesn't matter!*

Missy (Standard) Sizes
Typical Difference in Inches between Successive Sizes

Size Range	Bust	Waist	Hips
4, 6, 8	1	1	1
8, 10, 12	1 ½	1 ½	1 ½
12, 14,	2	2	2
14, 16, 18, 20	2 ½	2 ½	2 ½

Women's Sizes
Typical Difference in Inches between Successive Sizes

Size Range	Bust	Waist	Hips
16W, 18W, 20W	2 ½	2 ½	2 ½
20W, 22W, 24W, 26W	3	3	3

I've been told many times by customers that they "need a W size—a 'wide' size." "W" doesn't mean "wide." "W" actually stands for *"women's."* "Wide" is used to describe shoe sizes, *not* dress sizes.

Not all manufacturers follow the system portrayed in the foregoing tables. Some manufacturers use the following system for sizing their garments:

- Petite Small (also called "Extra Small")
- Small
- Medium
- Large
- Extra Large
- 1X
- 2X
- 3X
- 4X
- 5X

Please note that there also may be variations in these sizes, depending on the manufacturer. For example, an "Extra Large" by one manufacturer may correspond to "1X" by another manufacturer or a "Large" by yet another manufacturer. The universal truth is this: ***the size marked on the label is of no consequence—how the dress fits is the only thing that matters.***

It is important to note that many manufacturers produce women's clothing only in certain sizes. Most manufacturers do not produce garments in the full range of sizes, regardless of which system of sizes they use when designing their garments.

Foreign sizes are another matter. Sizes of women's clothing in Canada and the United Kingdom are different from those in the United States. Once again, trying on the garment is the most accurate way of determining which of these sizes will fit you the best.

The size of the average American has increased over the last two or three decades. Today the average American woman wears *approximately* a Size 14 dress. I say "approximately" because sizes vary from manufacturer to manufacturer as I have just explained. Because of this, it has become more and more difficult to find Sizes 2 and 4 in women's formal wear. Many designers begin at Size 6 or 8, which presents a real problem for the very small woman. Finding Size 0 dresses and Size 2 dresses is still a possibility in prom gowns but obviously this doesn't help MOBs and MOGs. In fact, it has now become easier to find formal clothing for plus-size women than for very small women. This is, in part, an indictment of the regulatory agencies that approve the ingredients that are added to our food, including high fructose corn syrup, which many people believe to be one of the most objectionable.

Petite Sizing

To me, this is such an important topic that it deserves a special section in this chapter.

It has been my experience that *a lot of women should be wearing petites and are not doing so.*

"Petite," contrary to what it sounds like, does not necessarily mean "small." In the clothing industry, it means *either* short-waisted *or* short-legged *or* <u>both</u>. If

42

you find that your jackets and tops buckle in the back, it means you need to wear a petite size.

A lady came into our store one day and I took one look at her and said, "You're a petite." "There's nothing petite about me!" she exclaimed. "You're a *women's* petite," I emphasized as I began to pull some dresses for her from the racks. After trying several on she exclaimed, "No wonder I've never been able to get anything to fit right! No one has ever told me this before."

Imagine being in your 50's and just discovering that you are really a 'petite!'

I'll never forget how shocked Terrie and I were when we were guests at the Best Dressed Women's Luncheon held annually here in Houston. We were surrounded by affluent attendees (not the honorees) wearing some of the most ill fitting clothes we'd ever seen. I have never seen so many jackets that buckled in the back! These were women who should have been wearing petite sizes but were not. Where do these very well-to-do women buy their expensive clothing? Is there no one there who is competent to help them when they are buying these high-priced clothes?

It is possible to be a long-waisted, short woman. This means that you can wear a missy (standard) jacket. This actually gives you many more options. Missy jackets are readily available in a wide range of styles, whereas the range of styles in petite sizes is more limited. With short legs you can most likely wear petite pants. Check to be sure the crotch-to-waist measurement (called the "rise" or "stride") of the pants is not too short. Since the only alteration you may need is to have the pants hemmed, this combination of missy jacket and petite pants is actually easier on the pocketbook. If you are short-waisted, altering jackets from missy to petite can be quite costly due to the labor involved.

Manufacturers have knowledge of fabrics and manufacturing techniques that we do not possess. Most of them are experts in their field. They know what fabrics lend themselves to a particular design and how the garment can best be constructed to take advantage of the characteristics of the particular fabric. Most of them are also extremely creative and are continually producing many excellent and varied and attractive designs and styles.

We, on the other hand, are in daily contact with mothers and observe their needs and hear their concerns and have been able to communicate this to some of the manufacturers. This is a synergy that has worked well for the manufacturers who have been open-minded enough to accept our suggestions and incorporate them into their designs.

As specialists in this field, we know what mothers need. We should—we work with them all day long, year in, year out. We know the "look" that mothers want. We also know what they don't want. We know what mothers feel comfortable about wearing and also what makes them look their best. We know what makes them look dowdy or matronly and what makes them look younger and slimmer. We also know the colors that will work best for our customers and the colors that won't work at all. Several of the manufacturers have recognized this and listened to us. We have been able to suggest changes, sometimes even small changes that have made some of their designs very successful. This has worked to their advantage and our customers' as we help mothers to look their best.

With the average size woman now being about Size 14, women's petites have become more available. As a matter of fact, Terrie and I have been instrumental in getting several of the well-known designers to make women's petite sizes. It took some effort, but eventually we were able to convince these designers that not all women who need petites are Size 8 or smaller! This is one of the more significant impacts we have had in the design of mothers' dresses. Until we urged the manufacturers to do this, few, if any, made petites in women's sizes. As a result, their success in this area has been remarkable.

It has become a continued source of pride and personal satisfaction for Terrie and me that we have had an important influence on some of the improved fashions that have evolved in mothers' dresses in recent years, giving mothers more and better choices.

Chapter 5

It's MY Day!

I have noticed a disturbing evolution in the years since I first opened my store. What seems to have evolved is the bride with the intense sense of "entitlement." "It's MY day!" And the rest of you be damned!

This attitude is evident in the way she treats her own mother, her mother-in-law-to-be, the bridesmaids, etc. Whatever happened to courtesy and respect?

Terrie was working with a bride and her mother in the dressing room when the bride exploded, "If you'd just lose that fat gut of yours, you'd look a lot better!!" Terrie was stunned. "You know," Terrie advised, "I'd be careful if I were you. The older I get the more I'm beginning to look like my mother and some of my female relatives, and I imagine your mother was your size when she was your age!" "I–I–was, I was!" stuttered the embarrassed mom. As bad as this is, believe me we've heard much worse. Most of us don't have the figure we had when we were first married, and the irony is that the birth of this child, has been a contributing factor.

I have seen women executives turn into bowls of jelly when confronted by a demanding and rude bride. "Well, it is *her* day!" is often the rationale. Not if your pocketbook is involved, and, personally, I don't think there ever is a day when disrespect is acceptable.

I've been known to pull mothers of the groom aside and caution them that they are allowing a dangerous precedent to get started. Disrespect and rudeness should never be allowed or tolerated.

Allowing oneself to become a doormat is not a temporary position. One mother confided, "It only gets worse once there are children involved. In order to see my grandchildren, I have to offer to cook dinner or clean her house!" You cannot be serious! How on earth was this ever allowed to start?!

God blessed my daughter and son-in-law with two adorable, bright boys. Terrie says that you know God has a sense of humor when he gave her boys instead of girls. (She has designed gowns for pageant contestants and winners, including the gown worn by Miss Texas when she won the title. She also selected some of the wardrobe for a former Miss Universe to wear to the events surrounding the contest.) No pretty prom gowns for Terrie—just tuxedos! Her brother in California, however, has the two girls. When I was cuddling the two-year-old, I whispered in her ear that Aunt Terrie could design her the most beautiful prom dresses. My son, who was standing nearby and overheard my whisper, informed me with finality, "Katya will *not* be going to prom!!"

Because she will some day be the mother of the groom, Terrie is particularly sensitive to the way mothers of the groom are often treated in our store. As the boys turned two, Terrie began shamelessly indoctrinating them that some day they would each find a wonderful girl who would love God first and would be very nice to their mommy! From some of the feedback we've gotten from the boys it appears to have made an impression. If either of the boys' fiancées were to be disrespectful to Terrie, I fully expect my son-in-law to take my grandson aside and let him know it was totally unacceptable. (We have a long time to wait, as the boys are now only six and ten!)

Contrary to the way many mothers of the groom are made to feel, they are *not* second-class citizens! Without them, there would be no groom and no wedding!

I have an incredibly close relationship with my daughter-in-law. Ours is a relationship of mutual respect. I was sensitive to her dreams for her wedding and I am sensitive and respectful of her opinions on how to raise my granddaughters. Obviously, we don't agree on everything, but never, for one moment, have we ever shown anything but respect for each other.

I'll never forget the mother of the groom who was an elementary school principal. This was a lady who obviously was a "take-charge" person. In my store, she became a "bowl of jelly" and allowed the bride to choose a color for her that was awful. No amount of persuasion on my part could convince the bride that this woman should be allowed to choose another color.

I did feel a sense of satisfaction when, two years later, this same mother returned for her daughter's wedding. This time, with no persuasion on our part, she chose a fabulous color.

My daughter was widowed at the age of thirty. When she was about to remarry several years later, she took the gown she planned to wear to a florist and asked her to design something to go with it. What the florist told her made a profound impression on me and set me to thinking.

"Terrie," she said, "At last I get to *use* my artistic ability! Every bride that comes in here tells me what she thinks she wants."

I started thinking about this and the implications. If I had to name flowers, I could probably name eight or so without much thought. A knowledgeable florist could probably name at least a hundred. If I restricted a florist to my eight, that would mean that I had ruled out the other ninety-two flowers, many of which could add so much more beauty.

I have observed that every bride tries to "re-invent the wheel." No one takes the wheel and makes a cart! Every bride tries to become a florist, a fashion designer, a calligrapher, a caterer, a musician, a baker, and so on. Rather than allowing professionals to do what they do best, these brides, with their limited knowledge, place restrictions on these professionals, thereby stifling their creativity. The result is a slight variation of a wedding they've attended, the expected, sometimes even the mundane. They've "re-invented the wheel"—not taken the wheel and made a cart!

Obviously, brides have "veto" power but by restricting these professionals, weddings seldom reach the esthetic and meaningful level they could reach. It's almost an incestual thing. A bride imitates the weddings she's attended, thereby seldom turning it into the unique and memorable event that guests will remember years later.

Chapter 6

I'm Not Happy About This Wedding!

Let's face it. Not every wedding is a happy occasion. Sometimes, the handwriting is on the wall and the marriage seems doomed from the start.

What's the old saying? "Love is blind!"

As a couple entered the store one day, I asked what their occasion was. "Our son's funeral," was the reply. Quickly, the mother corrected herself and said, "I mean wedding." It was, apparently, a Freudian slip! Her husband was not amused.

I regularly have repeat customers who will confide in me that the previous marriage lasted less than a year and now consider it was all a waste of time and money. I suggest that they concentrate, instead, on the good things about the wedding. Think of it as a great family reunion. Remember the relatives and friends who took time out of their busy lives to attend. Focus on all the positive and happy things that took place that day.

When you think of it, as parents, all we really want is for our children to be happy. If marrying someone we wouldn't choose actually makes our child happy, we still need to be supportive. If our child will not listen to our concerns and the marriage fails, we should stand by and help our child pick up the pieces of his or her life. It is important to create an atmosphere where our child can feel comfortable to come to us in time of hurt and grief. An "I told you so" attitude is not conducive to this.

Often, weddings are times when divorced parents of the bride or groom (or both) dread having to face each other. In my opinion this is a time for them to act like adults, suck it up and put smiles on their faces. They should fake it if necessary. I have encountered hundreds of brides and grooms through the years who are absolutely tied up in knots worrying about how their divorced or separated parents are going to act at their wedding. This is totally unacceptable! Parents and stepparents should reassure the bride and groom that they will, at least, be civil to each other.

I've worked with many mothers who will be coming face to face with their "replacement" who is only months older than the bride and sporting plastic surgery! Talk about pressure! I tell these mothers we need to find a "na, na-na, na, na" dress. "Something that will make him sorry he left you!"

Chapter 7

I'd Like To Be Able To Wear It Again

When Terrie and I go to the apparel market to select clothes for our store, we always discuss whether the dress in question has "an afterlife." No mother wants to buy a dress that she wears only once and then leaves hanging in her closet forever.

When we are selecting merchandise for our store, we take into consideration whether it *can* be worn again. Does it have an "afterlife"? Can it be shortened and made into a cocktail suit? Can it be worn on a cruise? What about New Year's Eve? How about an anniversary dinner? A gala? A ball?

One of the most unforgettable stories we've encountered was the lady who, in the course of looking for a dress to wear to her child's wedding, told us what had happened when her son got married. The bride's mother was very uncommunicative and would not give her any indication of what she planned to wear. Finally, two weeks before the wedding, in desperation, our customer decided she could wait no longer and would have to buy something. Out of frustration with the other mother's lack of communication, she chose a very expensive gown.

When filling her husband in on what she had done and how much it had cost, she said to him, "Don't worry. I'll get at least two wearings out of it. I'll wear it to the wedding and, when the time comes, you can bury me in it!"

Several weeks later, her housekeeper's son was getting married and this woman didn't have anything appropriate to wear. Since she thought so highly of this housekeeper, and since they wore the same size, she graciously offered to lend her housekeeper this lovely, expensive gown.

The wedding went off beautifully and her housekeeper looked fabulous. Shortly thereafter, and very unexpectedly, the housekeeper died. At the viewing, as our customer and her husband approached the casket, they were shocked to see that the housekeeper was dressed in *the borrowed gown!*

She said as they left in their car she told her husband, "Well, at least *someone* is being buried in it!"

It is not uncommon to hear some of our customers who are grandmothers exclaim, "After the wedding you can bury me in it!"

Not everything that happens in our store is humorous. Some of our experiences have been very poignant.

About two years after we opened the store, I got a phone call from a lady looking for a particular dress, in a particular color, to wear to her daughter's wedding. It was fuchsia and made of chiffon with a high neck and long sleeves. I was very familiar with the line she was looking for. In fact, by that time, we had become that designer's best small boutique customer.

The person on the phone explained that she had been very ill and needed a dress that had long sleeves in order to cover the bruises and needle marks on her arms. I encouraged her to come to our store and we would try to help her find something that would work.

Several hours later, she arrived with a friend. We showed her everything we had that would fit that description but nothing was exactly what she had envisioned. She was quite adamant about what she wanted, though in a very kind way.

We finally determined that the actual style she wanted had been discontinued by that designer and had, in fact, never been made in fuchsia.

Soon after they left the store, Terrie and I agreed that if we were that ill we would find an acceptable mother's dress and get on with it rather than add stress to our lives. "How important is a dress, really?" we said. Our point of view was about to change dramatically.

About an hour later, the phone rang and this time it was the friend. She explained that the reason this lady was so explicit about what she wanted was that she was terminally ill and also wanted to be buried in this dress. The high neck and long sleeves would cover the scars from the illness and fuchsia would brighten a complexion haggard from chemotherapy.

This phone call put the whole matter in an entirely different perspective. I immediately picked up the phone and called Miss Elliette, the designer, in Los Angeles, explaining the situation. Without hesitation, she said she would do it. She would find the pattern and even have it made in fuchsia. It would take several weeks.

When I called them back to let them know that we were going to be able to get the dress, they were thrilled.

Three weeks later, I received a call that our customer was in the hospital and things didn't look good. I immediately called Miss Elliette again and gave her the news. Within 36 hours the beautiful, fuchsia dress was in my store and the friend came quickly to pick it up.

Several days later, her friend called again and told me that "our" dress was on its way to Eternity, but not before this most gracious customer had written us a note thanking us for acquiring for her the dress she wanted more than any other.

In the course of a conversation one day, somehow the subject of funerals came up. This customer, with no hesitation, began to explain to me how she had made known all of her wishes regarding her funeral arrangements. Because I was a minister's daughter, I had been exposed to funerals and death at an early age and always, therefore, thought I had a rather mentally healthy view of dying, death and funerals. She surprised me as she went into great detail about her plans for the music, flowers, etc. "I even know what I want to be buried in," she continued. "I have this candy pink suit I absolutely adore, and I've told my husband that that's what I want to be buried in." And I thought *I* had a healthy view of this subject!

My mind began to race. She appeared to be in her early fifties and seemed to be in good health. She looked as though she could easily live at least another twenty-five years. I had no idea *what* size *I* might be in twenty-five years! How on earth did she? "Of course," she explained, "they'll have to slit open the back and sew in tics. I can't possibly wear *that* size anymore!"

We both burst into laughter!

Shortly after Terrie and I opened T. Carolyn, a mother, who worked in a mall department store, came in looking for a dress to wear to her daughter's wedding. She ended up choosing a very glittery gown.

Several days later she stopped by to tell us that, when her husband saw the gown, he proclaimed, "I guess I've got to take you on a cruise after the wedding!"

Wow! And I get to go on a cruise too?! (Cruises are a wonderful place to wear your mother's dress after the wedding!)

Chapter 8

What?!

One afternoon a very attractive, middle-aged woman entered my store. She was wearing a red leather mini-skirt, red sweater, red tights, red shoes and a number of gold chains. (The description sounds a bit garish, but, in reality, she looked quite fashion-forward at the time.)

She told me she was the mother of a groom. When I asked if she had something in mind, she paused and then said, "A slut dress! Do you have any slut dresses?" I could just see myself going to the apparel market and declaring, "I'd like to buy a dozen mothers' slut dresses, please!"

Suddenly, I remembered a dress my daughter had given me fits over when I ordered it. "You'll never be able to sell that to any mother," Terrie had admonished me. It had what I considered an "Elizabethan" neckline, a rounded, plunging neckline which would expose quite a bit of cleavage. Having grown up attending a British school, I had been exposed to a lot of Shakespeare, and I thought this neckline quite attractive. "Would you mind showing a bit of cleavage?" I asked this customer. "Heavens, no!" she exclaimed. "I'd love to show cleavage."

I brought out the dress, and it was a hit. While ringing up the sale, she explained to me that she was in the process of a very ugly divorce from a very abusive, alcoholic husband. The bride-to-be was an attorney and had chosen to side with the soon-to-be ex-husband, helping him to hide assets. I understood her anger.

As she walked out the door, dress in hand, she said, "I haven't heard the Catholic Church's stand on 'cleavage' but I guess I'll find out!"

Mothers are always telling me that they don't want to outshine the bride. I always tell them, that even if the bride were to wear sackcloth, it would be impossible to outshine the bride.

I had just told that to a customer when a voice came from the back of the store, "I've been to a wedding where the mother outshone the bride." She went on to explain that the mother, newly divorced, had shown up wearing a red sequined pageant gown with an extremely low, revealing neckline and a very wide, long slit up the front! Never in my wildest dreams could I have imagined someone showing up at a wedding in something like that!

I had finished working with a mother who was a Size 16. She was a short lady, and after several suggestions, we found something that really looked good on her. Standing back to get a good look at the "finished project," I advised her to wear a certain type of earring, as I felt this would complete the "look." "Oh, I never wear earrings!" she exclaimed. "My ears are too big!" "What?!" I exclaimed without hesitation. "Where on earth did you get that idea?" "From my brother," she said. "From the time I was a child, he always told me that I had big ears!"

This woman was in her fifties and had never worn earrings even though, believe me, there was nothing wrong with her ears!

We had a couple who both worked in a mortuary tell us that they were going to hold their wedding at the funeral home because they could get the chapel free of charge. They were going to use flowers already there for funerals and would make use of the piped-in music. Saving money must have been very important to them!

Perhaps one of the strangest requests was the mother who was looking for something Gothic to wear to her child's wedding. The wedding was on October 31 and happened to be on a Saturday. The bride had requested that all guests come in Gothic wear, velvet capes, etc. The wedding was being held in an older bed and breakfast and they were using caskets to hold the bottles of beer! The bride, not a young woman, was really into this vampire-type theme. She even had a car license plate that read, "Cruela"!

Speaking of strange, perhaps ridiculous is a better word—shortly before 9-11 a woman came to our store, fell in love with a particular design and wanted to order a dress in this style. There was just one problem—the manufacturer did not make this dress in her size. After a number of phone conversations, the manufacturer agreed to cut a pattern in her size and make a one-of-a-kind dress for this customer.

This was a most unusual concession on the part of the manufacturer, and even more so in view of the short delivery time required to meet the customer's scheduled wear date. They did it only because we were one of their best accounts and because we had such a good personal relationship with them spanning several years.

On September 12, with the wedding still three weeks away, the customer called and demanded to know if her dress was on its way. Terrie explained that the transportation system in the entire country was virtually at a standstill; all commercial air traffic had been grounded and, moreover, the site of manufacture was very close to the World Trade Center. The woman then became verbally abusive.

Her husband then called Terrie. Terrie explained to him, as she had previously explained to his wife, that planes were grounded and also the proximity of the manufacturing site to the World Trade Center. He, too, became verbally abusive and, get this, told Terrie that he was holding *her* personally responsible that his wife's dress was not on a plane that day, never mind the wedding was three weeks off and all civilian air traffic was grounded. We're happy that we've had no more customers like that.

One mother explained why she needed to find a black dress to wear to her son's wedding. The wedding invitation requested that all guests wear black as the bride "wanted to be the only one in white!"

A local photographer shared with me the story of a wedding that happened years earlier where everything that could go wrong did go wrong.

The bride and groom were both doctors. In the middle of the wedding, suddenly a very loud discordant noise began emanating from the organ. Apparently, the organist had suffered a fatal heart attack and had fallen into the pedals! When the cry, "Is there a doctor in the house?" was given, half of the congregation stood up! Eventually, the ceremony was started again, and the groom's grandmother positioned herself at the organ. She knew only one piece and it was not wedding music!

When the bride and groom exited the church, they discovered that the doors of the limousine were locked, the engine was running and the driver was gone! The driver had been in some sort of tiff with his employer and he had done this to retaliate. To get to the reception, the bride and groom had to ride in the photographer's new pick-up truck!

At the reception, it was discovered that the seating chart did not reflect the previously agreed seating arrangement. The mother of the groom was fuming. An error had been made during printing, but she was convinced that it had been done on purpose. The couple's honeymoon was in Italy. Something went wrong with their return tickets and they had to spend three days in the airport in Italy trying to get a flight back. However, when the photographer told me this story, he assured me that everything appeared to be going well, as, by then, the couple had been happily married for twelve years!

A repeat customer was waiting for a friend. As we exchanged pleasantries, I asked how the previous wedding had gone. "It was a disaster," was her reply. At first I thought she was joking. She then went on to explain. The couple had planned on scuba diving in the Caribbean on their honeymoon. The bride had taken scuba lessons just before the wedding and, apparently, she picked up some wicked virus from the pond where she had been taking these lessons.

The day of the wedding, the bride was dehydrated and extremely weak, almost passing out before the actual ceremony. They managed to get her down the aisle for the vows but then quickly got her into an ambulance, which had been called and was waiting outside the church. The groom rode in the ambulance that was taking his new bride to the hospital, while the groom's parents followed the ambulance in their car. The parents of the bride, meanwhile, went on to the reception to try to host the party. Throughout the reception, updates were given on the condition of the bride. There were no pictures of the wedding, the bride and groom never attended the reception, never saw the cake, never tasted the food!

Twenty-four hours later, the bride was released from the hospital still in her bridal gown and very weak, the groom still in his, by then, rumpled tuxedo. The bride was given a prescription to be filled. As the groom drove around attempting to find a pharmacy open in the middle of the night, he inadvertently went the wrong way on a one-way street. Suddenly, flashing lights from a patrol car appeared in his rear-view mirror. As the policeman peered into the car, he surmised that this couple was completely inebriated. To him, the bride looked as though she was almost unconscious and the groom looked very much under the weather. It took quite a bit of time for the groom to convince the police officer that things were not the way they looked and that they had just experienced a most hellacious previous 24 hours.

While attending a breakfast for local business owners at our bank, I found myself seated next to a plumber. When he found out the nature of my business, he told me about a recent incident his mother had told him about. It turns out that his mother, upon turning 60, decided to become a wedding consultant along with some of her friends, in a small town in East Texas where they lived. He informed me that this group of women had become known as the "Wedding Gestapo of East Texas."

He went on to relate that, at a recent wedding, just before the ceremony was to begin, the groom and best man, unfamiliar with the church, had gone in search of a restroom. They had climbed two flights of stairs with no luck. On the way down, they encountered a long hallway. Still in search of the elusive restroom, and with time running out, each decided to go in opposite directions. At the end of the hall, the groom opened the door and promptly fell into the baptistery, which was full of water! As the soft wedding music gently wafted through the church the serene setting was suddenly jolted with the unexpected sound of a loud splash. The vigorous undulations of the heavy curtains in front of the baptistery, which was behind the altar, left no doubt that someone had fallen in and was trying desperately to get out.

A murmur spread through the congregation, "What happened? Who is it?"

The plumber continued with his story. The best man quickly came to the rescue, fished the groom from the water, rounded up the groomsman nearest the groom's size, stripped him of his dry clothing and helped the groom dress quickly. As the wedding then continued, pretty much on schedule, a lone groomsman, not wanting to miss the ceremony, sat on the back row dressed only in his underwear!

At my own wedding, my brother was singing a solo, "I Will Lift up Mine Eyes" based on the 121st Psalm. As he sang the words "Steadfast we stand ..." I heard a loud collective gasp from the congregation followed immediately by a sickening "thump." I was afraid an elderly uncle of mine, who was attending our wedding, and who had a history of heart problems, had been stricken. I mouthed to my father, who was performing the ceremony, "Who is it?" Since he was facing the congregation, he just faintly smiled back at me.

It was a groomsman who had fainted and fallen backwards over the altar rail. As a child, he had contracted malaria in Africa where his parents were missionaries. Unbeknownst to us, he was recovering from a flare-up of malaria and had not been feeling well prior to the ceremony.

After the ceremony, I found out that ushers had quickly and quietly come down the aisle and carried the groomsman out to the fire station, which happened to be next door.

During the reception, a fireman appeared and said, "The groomsman is calling for his girlfriend, Barbara." "I hope not," was the reply. "Barbara just got married!" It turns out he was saying, "Barbara, I'm sorry. Barbara, I'm so sorry!"

A very lovely, elegant, obviously affluent lady and her daughter came into the store one afternoon and produced a sample of the material for the bridesmaids' dresses. It was a non-descript, mauvey-pink color, probably my least favorite color in the whole world for Caucasian women to wear.

The wedding was two weeks away. She said that she had several suits already that she had bought from one of the most expensive stores in Houston. She said that she was still looking, however, as she didn't think that she had yet found the 'perfect' dress. I advised her that she was a "winter" (something I could see that she already knew, but I wanted to let her know that I considered myself somewhat of a expert with colors). I told her that to look her best, she should wear something in the vivid jewel tones.

She expressed concern that the bright colors that I recommended would not go with the bridesmaids' dresses or the flowers.

I went into my standard information spiel. I reminded her that when the congregation saw her coming down the aisle, the bridesmaids would not yet have made their entrance. No one in the congregation would know yet what the bridesmaids were wearing. I asked her to picture herself walking down the aisle. On either side, there would be a sea of color consisting of women who would have gone to their closets that day and picked out what they looked best in. "Now," I asked her, "as the mother of the bride, shouldn't you do the same?"

The bride chimed in at this point. She said that, frankly, she didn't care how her mom looked in person, she only cared about the pictures. I explained that, if her mother did not look good in person, she couldn't possibly look good in the pictures! In this case, the camera does *not* lie!

"But I don't want to outshine the flowers!" the mom exclaimed.

"Exactly what flowers are you talking about?" I queried, trying to picture in my mind just what the problem was.

"The flowers up on the altar! We've spent $20,000 on the flowers, and I don't want to outshine the flowers!"

Will wonders never cease? Twenty thousand dollars and not wanting to outshine the flowers! I thought I'd heard it all. But I hadn't. There was more.

It turns out her daughter was marrying a minister's son. I am the daughter of a minister and my parents were also missionaries. The concept of $20,000 being spent on flowers for a wedding still jars my sense of priorities! My father would roll over in his grave if one of his children or grandchildren spent $20,000 on flowers for a wedding. Certainly, people spend a lot of money on flowers, but this was $20,000 in 1991!

My daughter, Terrie, was attending a wedding recently, in a lovely church in the city. Being somewhat of a musician herself, and coming from a family with many musicians, she always looks forward to the music at weddings.

As the soloist approached the altar, Terrie perceived that this lady had the air of a Beverly Sills, and she looked forward to what she thought would be a marvelous performance. To her amazement, the soloist began, "Mmmmemmmmmories," and came to an abrupt halt, as she was not in the same key as the accompanist. "B major," she commanded. "Mmmmmemories..." Again, she stopped. "D major," she bellowed, with the full mike on. "I don't know why you are having trouble with this," she admonished the bewildered accompanist. "We practiced this last night!"

On the third attempt, she got half way through the song and stopped abruptly, turned to the horrified, pony-tailed musician and admonished him again, informing him that they would have to start all over from the beginning. As he frantically attempted to modulate back to the beginning, she audibly huffed and puffed her indignation. It was obvious that the accompanist was a very skilled musician. Only a very skilled musician could have transposed from one key to another as masterfully as he had done. But the "deer-blinded-by-the-headlights" look on his face made it no secret he'd rather be any place but there, in that church, at that time.

"Beverly Sills" finally made it through the entire song. However, what puzzled Terrie most was that this woman's talent, or lack thereof, would not have qualified her for any church choir and, at best, she was no more than a mediocre congregational singer. Maybe she was a relative! Furthermore, who would choose the song 'Memories" for their wedding?! Had they *listened* to the *words*?

Couples sometimes pick the most inappropriate music for their weddings. One of my sisters-in-law, before she retired, was a professor of organ at a Mid-western university. She is a highly accomplished and very respected musician and also a recording artist. She has been known to refuse to play at weddings because she considered the music selected so inappropriate. At one wedding she was asked to play "Jeremiah Was a Bullfrog" for the recessional and she flatly refused to do it!

As a musician and as a daughter of a minister, I continue to be disappointed in the selection of music that many brides request and which I feel is totally inappropriate for a sacred ceremony. Through the years many of my customers have been organists and musicians who provide the music for weddings and also ministers' wives who are often accompanied by their husbands when visiting my store. When they find out my background, this subject always comes up. They, as do I, feel strongly that secular music has no place in a church or temple. It should be reserved for the reception.

One groom was patiently waiting for his mother to choose a dress, when the subject of funny stories came up. He told me of the wedding where he was a groomsman. It was an outdoor wedding and they were near the gazebo awaiting the bride. Unfortunately, a restroom door opened to the outside very close to where they were standing. Just as the bride was about to make her entry, the restroom door flew open and a very young boy emerged, pants down around his ankles, yelling, "I need some help!"

A visiting minister, wanting to have a few minutes to pray in solitude before the ceremony, wandered down the hall of the church. He opened a door and unwittingly found himself in a closet that could not be opened from the inside! As the minutes ticked by and the minister was not in his appointed place, concern began to rise. Eventually, someone heard loud banging coming from a closet in a remote section of the church. They opened the door and a very sweaty, embarrassed "man of the cloth" was released from his involuntary self-confinement. I think the biblical exhortation about going into your closet to pray, should be followed only if you're certain you can also get back out of the closet!

An incident that haunts me to this day was the mother and grandmother from Louisiana who visited our store in search of the grandmother's dress. The mother of the bride explained that she, herself, was terminally ill and that the bride had booked the cathedral in Jackson Square in New Orleans where there was a two-year waiting list for weddings. Because of this, her daughter's wedding was still 18 months away. This mother, knowing that she would not be alive in 18 months, had brought her own mother to our store to help her pick out her dress for the wedding. She explained that she wanted to know what her mother (the bride's grandmother) would be wearing since she, the mother of the bride, wouldn't be there to see it. Wouldn't you have thought that they would have rescheduled the wedding to an earlier time, cathedral or not, so that this mother would have been able to attend her own daughter's wedding?

A minister, who is a friend of mine told me about a wedding in which he was participating. The officiating minister had just received a new pair of bi-focal glasses. As he approached the position at the altar where he was to stand, he tripped on the step and fell forward, arms outstretched, knocking over the candelabra! Immediately, small fires from the candles erupted on the carpet. Guests hurriedly ran up onto the altar and began to stomp out the fires. The minister was so mortified he ran back into the church office and began weeping. "I've ruined their wedding! I've ruined their wedding!" he sobbed. With the officiating minister unable to regain his composure, my friend ended up having to perform the entire ceremony!

More than thirty-five years ago, I was the organist for a wedding in Anchorage, Alaska. As the actual ceremony began, I quietly amused myself by looking at the guests, the flowers, the bride, etc. Suddenly, I was jarred back to the moment when I was sure that I heard the minister asking the bride if she promised to "Love, honor, and *serve*." On the edge of the organ bench, every hair on the back of my neck standing straight up, I listened intently as the groom was asked to repeat his vows. There was **no** "serve" in his vows! Using every bit of self-control I could muster, I restrained myself from laying both arms across the organ's manuals and thereby interrupting the ceremony with a highly audible protest.

The minute the ceremony was over, I rushed to the side of the minister, who happened to be a friend, and asked him if I had heard correctly? "Now, now, Barbara. Don't get upset. It only means serving her husband a TV dinner on Friday nights!"

I'm sure if he continued to use that phrase in the future, he remembered my female indignation! I hope he removed it! Of course, we know that this type of vow was once more common than it is today, but it always made me bristle.

Several weeks before my niece's wedding, she asked if I would help with some of the final arrangements. I was happy to do so. One of my tasks was to arrange for a horse and carriage to take the newlyweds for a romantic ride around nearby Hermann Park after the reception. As the wedding ceremony and reception were to be held in a hotel, and the couple was to spend their first night of wedded bliss in the same hotel, an exit in a horse and carriage was to be a fitting ending to a perfect evening.

As the time approached when the couple was to leave the reception, I went out to check on the horse and carriage and discovered that the hotel's shuttle bus was parked directly alongside the carriage which was waiting right in front of the hotel entrance. Concerned about the composition of the photographs, I went in search of someone who could move the shuttle. From bellman, to concierge, to valets, I had no success. Finally, the manager found the keys and proceeded to the area where the shuttle was parked.

At the very moment the bride and groom were attempting to climb into the carriage, the bus started backing up. The beeping of the vehicle-in-reverse warning signal spooked the horse and he began to rare up. The carriage driver, who had been standing nearby to assist the couple into the carriage, grabbed the reigns and was immediately lifted off the ground by the unruly horse. Guests, who had come to witness their departure, could only frantically shove the bride and groom into the carriage, as it started off at a fantastic speed, with the driver still scrambling into his seat and trying to regain control of the horse.

Since everything happened so quickly and so unexpectedly, no pictures were taken of their departure. As the official photographer had to leave at this point, I asked my husband if he would position himself at the front door and await their return and attempt to get at least one picture of the bride and groom in the carriage.

When they had not returned after an hour and a half, we all became concerned. The ride around the park was to have taken less than an hour.

It seems the carriage driver, a recent immigrant from a northern European country, had misunderstood the instructions and instead of taking them for a slow, romantic ride around Hermann Park, had briskly headed off in the direction of another hotel in downtown Houston. My niece became concerned when she realized they were heading away from the park. Her attempt to communicate with the driver was to no avail. Their route took them through the seamier side of downtown Houston. At one point, as the carriage approached an underpass, they spotted several shadowy figures crouched in the darkness. As the carriage stopped for a traffic light, these homeless people all surged forward intent on seeking a handout. This was a side of Houston's nightlife to which they had not previously been introduced! My niece's immediate thought was for the expensive watches they had given each other for wedding presents.

As the carriage pulled up to one of the older hotels in Houston, the staff, thinking that my niece and her husband had come there to spend their wedding night, greeted them enthusiastically. The groom explained what had happened and that they needed a ride back to their hotel. The carriage driver offered to take them back but his offer was quickly declined. Stranded in a strange hotel, still wearing his tux, the groom had not a penny on his person and certainly not a quarter for a pay phone (these were the days before the ubiquitous cell phone). He had to ask the hotel staff to let him use the phone at the reception desk. His first call was to us, but was incorrectly put through to another guest, who, upon being woken from his deep slumber, was virtually incoherent. The next call was correctly put through to our room but went unanswered because we were, by then, back at the hotel entrance anxiously awaiting their return.

Going down his mental checklist, he called his best man who, after the evening's festivities, was, by now, at home recuperating in the hot tub with his wife and a few other wedding guests. Since they were best friends, the best man was fully convinced, initially, that the groom was trying to play a practical joke on him. Finally, he realized that this was no joke. He was being asked to drive to the downtown hotel and rescue the stranded couple.

It was now past midnight. My husband, the substitute photographer, who by now began fearing the worst, paced back and forth while anxiously waiting for the carriage that never returned. Eventually, however, a car inconspicuously pulled up at a different entrance to the hotel, and out stepped the windblown bride and groom. Consequently, because they did not return to the entrance whence they departed, their arrival back at the hotel, like their departure, was not photographed either!

When I ran into them in the corridor of the hotel moments after their return, the bride had her veil in hand and her hair was disheveled and the groom looked a little the worse for wear.

Always trying to make lemonade out of lemons, I asked the couple if they couldn't have just relaxed and enjoyed the ride. Apparently, the uncertainty about their destination together with the smell of a sweaty horse mingling with the smell of the "potty bag" under the horse's tail were conducive to neither relaxation nor enjoyment. The next day, before my niece and her husband left for their Caribbean honeymoon, we spoke on the phone and she recounted their experiences of the previous night's ride. As we ended the conversation, she said to me, "Thanks a lot, Aunt Barbara. That was the ride from *hell!*"

Recently, for the first time in years, I saw my college roommate. When I told her about this book, she told me of the gaff at her nephew's wedding.

This was not the groom's first wedding and his mother was less than enthusiastic about the event. Entering the restroom with a friend, prior to the ceremony, she was expounding at length about his previous failed marriage, saying that she sure hoped "that this marriage would go better than the last one." "I'm sure it will," was the reply coming from an adjacent stall. "My daughter is the bride!" What's the old saying? "Walls have ears."

A former bridal consultant told me of a wedding in which she was assisting. The mother of the bride had rushed to the restroom just prior to the ceremony. Due to her haste, she unknowingly caught the back of her chiffon skirt in her panty hose. She proceeded down the aisle totally unaware that her undergarments and the back of her thighs were completely exposed. When the consultant realized what was happening, she literally ran down the aisle behind the mother, and successfully released the dress before the mother reached her seat.

Lesson learned: *Check the back of your dress, as well as the front, before you leave the restroom, no matter how rushed you are!*

A mother told us of her own experience at the wedding of one of her children. She had bought a new pair of shoes for the occasion. Because her left foot was slightly larger than her right, and because she was in a hurry, she only tried on the left shoe. Dressing at the church, just before the wedding, she discovered, too late, that the shoebox contained *two* left shoes. As uncomfortable as it was, she had no other option but to wear both left shoes as she walked down the aisle!

While checking out at the register, the customer, who had been a soloist at many weddings, told me of one where expense had not been a consideration. In fact, she estimated that the father had spent over $100,000 on the wedding.

The little ring bearer spent the entire time during the ceremony literally somersaulting up and down the steps of the altar, with no attempted intervention by his mother. At the same wedding, one of the bridesmaids threw up while standing at the altar! This reminds me of the saying, "The best laid plans of mice and men ..."

I am a firm believer that, with small children's short attention span, they cannot be expected to stand at the altar for 15 or 20 minutes while the ceremony is in progress without becoming a distraction. Often, their only function is to be a part of the processional. In this case, once the wedding party takes its place at the altar, these children need to be seated in the congregation with a parent or responsible adult. The best solution to this problem, that I have seen, is having a relative placed near the front, on the aisle, and as the child/children approach, they are unobtrusively "whisked" onto the pew next to the relative who can keep them occupied during the ceremony. As soon as the ceremony is completed, the children are "released" and they join the recessional. Picture taking is another story!

A grandmother told us about her little grandson who was participating as the ring-bearer. As the little boy proceeded down the aisle, he began making a muted but audible noise. As he approached the altar, he became more self-assured and the noise became louder. The entire congregation, at that point, was giggling. When questioned after the wedding, he explained that he was the Ring Bear and everyone knows that *bears* growl!

Remember, Murphy's Law ("If *anything* can go wrong, it *will* go wrong") is alive and well at *every* wedding. It is maliciously lurking around every corner, waiting only for an opportunity to prove its malevolent existence.

Chapter 9

Color, Color, Color!
The Importance of Color

I have my own rule about the three most important things to be considered in choosing a dress.

They are: color, color and—yes, you guessed it—COLOR!

I simply can't overemphasize the importance of color! I have seen color transform women who look "average" into women who look beautiful! A style that flatters your figure or disguises its defects is extremely important, but color is the single most important consideration. If I were forced to choose between the two, I would choose color. I say this because, no matter how perfect the style may be for your figure, you will *never* look good if it is the wrong color. Your *dress* might look beautiful, but *you* will not. Remember: our number one goal is to make *you* look beautiful!

Naively, before opening our store, I thought that fabrics were made in the same colors every year. Was I ever wrong! I came to find out that colors are selected years in advance by an international association representing a wide range of industries. They are the ones who are given the responsibility for choosing the colors for fabrics, appliances, cars, upholstery, paint, etc. Those of us who are old enough can still remember green bathtubs and copper-tone refrigerators. People whom you and I have never even met chose those colors for us! This explains why you may go several years and not see a particular item in a particular color, and why some colors are "in" and some are "out."

This creates a real problem for many African-American weddings. It has been common in the African-American culture that the mothers wear the colors chosen by the bride-to-be as her "wedding colors." This is fine, but the problem arises when fabrics in those colors are not being manufactured that year! To make matters even worse, I've worked with many brides who are asking their mothers to wear a *particular shade* of that color, making it even more impossible to find. The problem is further compounded when the mother is asked to wear a color that is really not a good color for her. I'm pleased that I'm beginning to see more brides straying from this tradition. It really is in the best interest of the mothers, as well as the bride, for the mothers to look their best.

Color is an interesting thing. And so is how people perceive themselves in different colors. One Size 32W lady informed me that she "just wanted to blend, didn't want to stand out." With as much tact and as kindly as I could, I informed her that there was no way she was going to "blend." If she wore an unflattering, pastel color, she would look larger than she was and people would think, "Boy, there's a large lady!" But if she wore something in a "dynamite" color, people would think, "My, she looks nice!"

"Now, which do you choose?" I asked. She chose to go with "dynamite."

During the course of trying to determine the color the mother thinks she is looking for, I have been shown many things: paper napkins, pieces of thread, petals from a silk flower, yards of ribbons, paint chips, pictures that didn't print quite right, shoes, hats, pieces of jewelry, etc.

The one that stands out in my mind was the mother who systematically listed off every possible thing connected with the wedding and its color. Finally, she took a deep breath and reached into her purse and pulled out a jagged piece of carpeting measuring approximately 4 inches by 6 inches. "And this," she exclaimed, "is a sample of the carpet in the church!"

Suddenly a vision of mothers cutting out their sample of the carpet flooded my mind. I could see it clearly. Your child announces the engagement and the next Sunday, quietly, and as discreetly as possible, with probably a manicure scissors or a small penknife, you reach under the pew and begin to cut out your sample! I immediately envisioned churches across this nation whose carpet looked as though giant moths had invaded the church and left behind jagged, gaping holes. The look of horror on my face left this mother puzzled.

"Is this piece of carpet actually from the church?" I stammered. "Oh no," she said. "We happen to have the same color of carpeting at home and I had some scraps laying around." I sighed an audible sigh of relief.

Shortly after we'd opened the store in 1991, we had a lady come in asking for the "brightest" color we could find. It turned out that four years before, when her daughter was getting married, she wore a pale pink dress.

She told us that when she saw the pictures, she actually cried. The problem? She didn't show up in the pictures!

Another customer of ours, a few weeks after her son's wedding, returned to our store to show us pictures of the wedding. She was a redhead and we had encouraged her to choose a green dress. The other mother, in this out-of-state wedding, had chosen pale pink. I saw firsthand what the previous mother meant. It was as though the other mother wasn't in the picture! It was impossible to describe anything about her dress. It was even impossible to see where her hair ended and her dress began! Nothing! It was like "Casper the Friendly Ghost"!

Had I been thinking, I would have asked for a copy, and it would have served me well through the years as I've tried to explain to women how important color is. I was so shocked by this picture, I called a friend, who is a photographer, and explained what I had seen, or in this case, not seen. Photographers use the term "exposure" to mean the amount of light reaching the photographic film. He explained that, the lighter the color of the garment, the more light it reflects back to the camera. This causes overexposure in that area of the photograph that results in a "washed out" effect with significant loss of detail, while the rest of the photograph is perfectly exposed.

I have had many an interesting conversation with photographers over the years. The upshot of all these conversations is this: do not, for one second, think that the camera will see exactly what you see. There has never been a camera made that can duplicate the natural vision we humans have. Our brain takes the information conveyed to it from the eye and, after complex processing within our brain, produces the image that we "see." Because of this, scientists tell us we don't actually see with our eyes, we see with our *brain*. Our brain makes all sorts of compensations that a camera cannot make. This explains why *something that may look good to you may not show up well in a photograph*. This is why the mother who wore pale pink hardly showed up in the photographs described above.

What's the old saying, "The camera doesn't lie"? In many ways this is true. But this is also a fact: *Sometimes the camera cannot tell the truth!* This is also why it is so important to select colors that not only look good on you, but also colors that will *photograph well*. Remember this: *In some colors you will always look better in the mirror than you will in the photographs*. For example, the mother who wore pale pink, and who was just described, almost certainly looked worse in the photographs than she did in person, otherwise she probably wouldn't have purchased the dress to begin with. (This reminds me of the compliments I would receive years ago when I wore an ivory colored pantsuit. Yet in photographs, I looked like a beached whale!!)

In the beginning of Chapter 1, I wrote about the neutral colors, brown, green and blue. These are nature's colors. We see them all the time—the blue sky, the green hills, the brown earth. Yet every week I have mothers ask if a certain color is appropriate for a certain season. For example, a mother will ask me, "But since I'll be wearing this in the summer, can I really wear brown (or red or green or bright blue)? Shouldn't I be wearing a soft, cool pastel?" What colors are the flowers of summer? Are they soft pastels? Very few are! Most are brilliant colors. I think Terrie put it most succinctly when she said, "You don't stop wearing your best colors because of the season. You just change the weight of the fabric instead." In selecting your dress, *always* choose your *best color* in a style that is most flattering to your figure. Choose the *weight* of the fabric based on the season.

When all you have left after the wedding are the pictures, it is extremely important to choose colors that will photograph well. Mothers of the bride who wear champagne, ivory or very light colors run the risk of having no distinction between their dress and the bride's gown, culminating in a "hot air balloon with two beige faces" look. It's not the look we recommend!

My son in-law, who for several years worked in the print industry, has told me that certain pale colors have to be computer-enhanced *several times* to even show up! Unfortunately, the pictures you see in catalogs and in advertising have been "doctored" and are *not* the "real thing."

I remember watching a television show several years ago, where Sally Jesse Raphael told of going to a party where some of the world's top models were being honored. She did not recognize any of them. Because their pictures had all been so "enhanced," these women didn't look like their pictures. The really terrible thing about this is that we have a nation of women and teenage girls trying to look like people who don't even exist!

One busy Saturday, the bride, future bridegroom, her mom and dad dropped by the store looking for bridesmaids' dresses. I quickly explained that we don't handle bridesmaids' dresses but focus on mothers. The bride seemed to want my opinion anyway and asked what I would suggest for bridesmaids' dresses, as it was going to be an outdoor wedding. I told her that if she were to choose a color that looked good on all of the girls, they would be eternally grateful and the pictures would be better. This is why I suggest to brides that they take a picture of the bridesmaids' dresses before making a final decision. Six weeks after the wedding is a little late to find out that the color chosen doesn't photograph well. I don't sell bridesmaids' dresses, but this is my "free advice." I went on to expound on the colors I believe look good on everyone. I added that peach, for example, looks awful on most girls. In fact, it can make most women look sallow and jaundiced.

The bride flinched as though I had hit a nerve. I was taken aback, since I had understood that they were still in the planning stages and that nothing had been purchased yet. "What's wrong?" I queried. "I thought you hadn't picked out your bridesmaids' dresses yet." "We haven't," she confirmed. "But my fiancé thought that peach would be a really pretty color on the grass." "Forget how it looks on the grass!" I exclaimed. "Think of how it looks on the girls!" They immediately broke into laughter and realized the folly of his reasoning.

During a particularly busy afternoon, Terrie called me away from the computer to help on the floor. A lady who was to be the only attendant in her niece's wedding was looking for a burgundy, floor length gown. She had red hair. I asked her if the niece had asked her to wear burgundy or if it was her idea. I was somewhat amazed when she informed me that the bride had already bought burgundy paper napkins and thought a burgundy gown would go with the napkins. I gently explained that the color of paper on tables should have no bearing on the choice of an attendant's dress. Especially when this color would not look good on her, I was even more amazed when she told me that the bride had informed her that she, as the maid of honor, would be carrying red roses down the aisle! As diplomatically as I could, I showed her what red roses would look like against the burgundy gown.

It was at this point she decided that she'd better call the bride long distance and discuss the possibility of a *green* gown. A few hours later, she returned to purchase a green gown.

I am always surprised that some women remark to me that they can't wear a certain color because they wore that color to their *other* child's wedding. My response is this: if it's your best color, why would you want to go for your second best look? Looking fantastic should be the goal!

Often, when trying to make a point about color, I will put the customer in front of the mirror and do what I call the "blink test." Holding one color up to her face, I will ask her to memorize what she sees and then ask her to close her eyes. Then I will hold up the other color to her face and ask her to open her eyes. Immediately, it will become obvious which color is better—and it only took thirty seconds!

In my opinion the colors that look good on everyone are teal-blue, turquoise and usually royal blue.

At the risk of sounding repetitive, I'm going to say again:

- One of the most difficult concepts that I have had to get across to mothers, as well as brides, is this: mothers are **not** part of the wedding party. They are **not** expected to match the bridesmaids' dresses. Mothers are **not** senior bridesmaids!

- Traditionally, the mother of the bride is the hostess of the wedding, and the mother of the groom is the most honored guest. As such, they should be better dressed than the other guests.

Since this is usually the second most photographed event in the mother's life, it only makes sense that she should choose the color she looks best in and the color that will photograph best.

Matching or blending with pew bows and altar flowers makes *no* sense when she is sitting on the second pew of the church surrounded by a rainbow of color—a rainbow of guests who went to their closet that day and chose what they look best in.

For goodness sake, shouldn't the mothers do the same?

One day, a Size 22 lady came through the door telling me she wanted a pink dress to wear to her daughter's wedding. Pale pink in a Size 22 makes a woman look like a 32 in photographs, and besides, this woman was a "winter." She needed jewel tones.

"What color are the bridesmaids' dresses?" I asked.

"Red," she replied.

"Then you'd look great in a blue," I said.

"I need a *pink* dress," she persisted.

"But with the red bridesmaids' dresses, you'd look so much nicer in blue," I advised.

"Look," she said with a tone of exasperation rising in her voice, "I'm the mother of the bride and the mother of the bride wears pink, the mother of the groom wears blue!"

"What???" Terrie and I both exclaimed in unison.

With a stomp of her foot, she repeated her statement. In fact, she was so emotional at this point that Terrie and I backed off.

"Look ... you can wear any color you want, but we've never heard of this before."

A couple of seconds passed. She looked a little bewildered and then explained, "It's a Polish wedding. In a Polish wedding, the mother of the bride wears pink, and the mother of the groom wears blue. When the people at the wedding see me in pink, they'll know that I'm the mother of the bride."

For one brief moment, I thought it was a joke!

"What happens if a guest shows up at a Polish wedding wearing pink or blue?" I asked Terrie later. "I suppose guests know better than to show up at a Polish wedding wearing pink or blue!!" she said.

I hope this anecdote has not offended anyone who is Polish or is of Polish ancestry. This was never my intention but, if such a practice ever existed, for the sake of the mothers, I do hope that it no longer does.

If I had a dollar for every mother of the groom who tells me she's heard her role at the wedding is to *"wear beige and keep her mouth shut,"* I could retire financially secure! That cliché is from the dark ages! I think it's actually meant to indicate how little control the mother of the groom has over the actual wedding plans. However, I think that has begun to change in recent years.

With equal rights, come equal rights for mothers of the groom! Having raised a son myself, I'm here to tell you, mothers of the groom have been through enough to be entitled to have some say about what they wear to their own son's wedding. Trust me! "And besides," I tell mothers of the groom, "If you look closely, the bottom line of the Equal Rights Amendment says in the smallest of print, *'Mothers of the groom are equal too'*!"

Having been a musician at lots of weddings, I thought I'd seen it all and knew it all, but I was wrong! The first time a customer came into my shop and told me they were having a black and white wedding, I thought they meant bi-racial! I didn't realize they meant the bridesmaids were wearing black and white dresses. I soon came to realize that weddings are often referred to in terms of the color of the bridesmaids' dresses. Often, they'll say, "We're having a black and white wedding" or, "We're having a burgundy and silver wedding," etc.

There are also considerations I would never have thought of. One mother of the bride brought two of her friends along to give their advice. She asked them what they thought of the color of the dress she had on. "It looks great," one said, with utter conviction. "And besides, that color will go with whatever color your hair is at the time of the wedding!"

Only after opening our store have I come to realize the emotions involved in choosing colors.

One sweet-spirited lady told me why she hated the color blue. While they were in mid-conversation, her mother, who, at the time, was at the hospital undergoing chemotherapy, suffered a massive heart attack. Hearing the nurses calling out "Code Blue," and the trauma of watching the futile attempts to revive her mother, left her with an intense emotional dislike of anything blue.

Another time, a mother who was a pretty redhead, was standing in front of the big mirrors in our store, trying to decide on a color. She had brought her mother with her, and both of us encouraged her to go with the green dress. All the customers in the store at that time weighed in with their opinions and without exception, it was green. She ended up buying the green.

A few days later when she came back into the store to pick up a pair of earrings, she confided that she had figured out why she had hesitated over the green. It was because she was a nurse and she worked in green scrubs all day long. My reaction to that was, "You're darn lucky you get to work in your best color. Think of those horrible mustard-yellow jackets Century 21 made their people wear for years!"

Another lady informed me, that the dress I thought would be perfect for her was the exact color of the dress her grandmother was buried in. So, since the age of four, she had associated that color with the death of her grandmother.

I'll never forget the time a lady came into our shop exclaiming that she would buy anything but a purple dress. I was startled, as I had observed that she was a "winter" and purple was one of her very best colors. She had dark hair, fair skin, and blue eyes.

She tried on several dresses. Then, with some coaxing on my part, agreed to try on some purple ones, even though she made it perfectly clear she did not intend to buy purple. Every time she had on a purple dress, other customers in the store volunteered that she looked great. I couldn't understand her negative emotional involvement with the color purple. I half jokingly asked her if her mother had beaten her with a purple belt. "No," she told me, but she said she knew why she disliked the color purple. Back in the second grade, she'd had a teacher who had been very mean to her, and this teacher always wore purple. Hence, ever since, she has hated the color purple! "Why do you allow this 'rotten educator' to deprive you of looking *your best* in a color that happens to be *your best*?" I implored. "You know, you're right!" she exclaimed, and left my shop with a PURPLE dress! It was like a trip to the shrink! (Teachers, take note! You are having a profound influence on your students. Please make sure it is a *positive* influence!)

Terrie showed a mother of the groom a purple dress because she thought both the color and style would look good on this lady. She informed Terrie that she could not wear purple because she felt it might antagonize her daughter-in-law-to-be who was still upset over her fiancé's ex-girlfriend's wedding. Either by sheer coincidence or vindictive planning, the ex-girlfriend had chosen the identical bridesmaids' dresses, in the identical color and identical pattern and the identical flowers that this bride had chosen. The mothers at that wedding had both worn purple, so this mother felt it might upset the bride if she chose purple. Terrie asked if the same guests would be attending her son's wedding, and the mother said "No." Talk about walking on eggshells!

More frequently than I care to think of, mothers of the groom will tell me that they've been told to wear a particular color. My immediate response is, "God spoke to you?" "Might as well have been," is often the reply. "Mothers are **never** told what to wear," I counter. "*Bridesmaids* are told what to wear."

My theory as to how this often happens is this: the mother of the groom, in an attempt to be congenial and to appear easy to get along with, asks the bride what she should wear. The bride has little, if any, experience in planning a wedding. But, by the very nature of the question, she assumes that this must also be a decision she is expected to make. So, she pulls a color out of the air. By doing this, the mother of the groom has, in fact, laid a trap for herself. Very seldom does a bride hold fast with her color "command" once I've been able to explain to her the realities of how color impacts a wedding. In cases like this, she usually ends up telling the mother to wear whatever she feels good in and looks best in.

A couple of years after we had opened the store, I received a telephone call from a gentleman. He was obviously calling from a pay phone near a busy intersection, as I could hear the noise of the traffic in the background. He asked if I sold a certain designer's clothes. I did. He then asked if I had anything in mauve. I informed him that I could get just about any color, but, if his wife was Caucasian, I generally didn't recommend the color mauve. "But I love her in mauve!" he exclaimed.

Later that day, they arrived at my store. He was still emphatically proclaiming how good his wife looked in mauve. Quietly, I began to pull some dresses for her, one of which was mauve. They had to buy two dresses because the wedding was out of state and they were hosting a reception back here in Houston at a later date.

Two hours after arriving at my store, they purchased a royal blue dress and a purple dress! She told me later, with great delight, that she had never before received as many compliments as she did in her royal blue and purple dresses. "I guess I've just been wearing the wrong colors all these years!" she concluded.

This same husband declared that he was so financially and emotionally exhausted from this wedding, that he had informed his other son that he couldn't *even date* for the next two years! The thought of another wedding was just too much to bear!

For women of African descent, mauve is magnificent, as are champagne and light pink. However, for Caucasian women, mauve is so near skin tone color that they might as well wear nothing! It completely drains all color from their faces and makes the individual look

25 pounds heavier in photographs. This achieves the ultimate in "matronly," in my opinion.

Asian women, as well as many Hispanic women, look their best in the bright, clear jewel tones— royal blue, red, and purple. Most women from the Middle East also need the vibrant, clear colors such as browns and golds, but greens tend to make their skin appear sallow. Interestingly enough, I have found that burgundy, often called eggplant or aubergine, really looks best on a woman with very fair skin, very dark hair and eyes. For those of us living in the South, our skin is exposed to enough sunlight that burgundy tends to make us look orange. It is a difficult color for a lot of people to wear.

It is important to realize that throughout one's lifetime the color of one's skin, hair and sometimes, even one's eyes will change. As a result, colors that look best on you will also change. This is why it is important to constantly analyze both *your makeup* and *the colors that you wear*. I am keenly aware of this. I recently stopped coloring my hair and have allowed it to return to its natural color, which is *now* mostly gray. Currently, I find myself with a closet full of clothes and shoes that are no longer my best colors.

I must confess this has come as quite a shock to me. With hazel eyes and dark blonde hair, the warm tone colors of green, brown, gold, etc., have always been my best colors. Coral lipstick and coral nail polish had been my color of choice for more years than I choose to admit. With a preponderance of gray hair, in various shades, I find that the cooler colors of plum, burgundy, navy, blue-red, white, silver and black (when enhanced by a brighter color) have now become my colors of choice. My coral lipstick and nail polish has been replaced with shades of pink. I've gone from being an "autumn" to being a "winter"! Even more dismaying, is my closet full of brown shoes and purses! As a further point of interest, when I recently traded in my olive-green car, I chose to replace it with a *burgundy* car, a color I never would have chosen before!

One day a zealous sales rep was trying unsuccessfully to sell me on a "new" color for the upcoming spring. It was a pale, nondescript color. I politely remarked that the color would not show up in the wedding photographs and furthermore, it was not a good color on anyone. "Aw, come on, Barbara," he pleaded. "It's a beautiful color." "It sure is," I countered, "for walls, carpets and upholstery. Just not on people! Look, Fred," I continued, "Hold this sample up to your face and look into the mirror. Tell me what you see." "Well, it doesn't look to-oooo bad," he replied. "You expect *me* to sell, 'not to-oooo bad' to *my* mothers?!" I retorted.

One year, navy suddenly became *the* color. The designers and manufacturers called to give me the good news. Immediately, I asked, "And what about the black tuxedos?" "My God! We never thought of that!" was their reply. Now, I'm not a rocket scientist, but *I* sure thought of that! Think how upset your husband is when he discovers that he's worn one black sock and one navy sock to work!

In the course of trying to advise mothers, we always ask what the bridesmaids will be wearing.

Occasionally, when the color "navy" comes up, I always encourage the bride to choose navy tuxedos. Often they will respond, "We're using navy vests with the black tuxes." Hello! Get back with me when you find yourself on your way to somewhere and you suddenly notice you've grabbed your navy shoes and you're wearing them with your black dress! The problem with navy blue and black is, that when worn in close proximity to one another, they look like a "near miss."

I think of all the repercussions that colors can have. I guess my background of having been at so many weddings as an organist and vocalist, my having put on musicals as a music teacher, and having dressed so many mothers has made me acutely aware of this. The number of people in the bridal and special-occasions business selling things without realizing the consequences, or sometimes, even worse, not caring, never ceases to amaze me.

One morning, I was going through my customary interrogation of a mother preparing for her child's wedding. I ended my questioning with, "And what color are you wearing when you get the most compliments?" She looked startled, almost as if she'd never received a compliment. To shorten the pregnant pause, I looked to her husband and asked, "What is your wife wearing when she gets the most compliments?" "Zip, nada, nothing!" was his immediate reply. "She's wearing absolutely nothing—she's totally NUDE!"
I have stopped asking husbands that question!

One morning, I answered the phone and found myself talking to a customer who had been in the store the day before. She told me that her husband hated the color of the dress she had chosen. When I realized which customer I was talking to, I was flabbergasted. She had chosen a fabulous dress in a fabulous color. I reminded her that unbiased customers had stopped and raved about how good she looked. "How do you feel about your choice?" I asked. "Oh, I love the dress and the color," she replied. "What do you think the problem is then?" I asked. "Well," she responded with a pause, "My husband *is* color blind." "Are *all* your guests at the wedding going to be color blind?" I asked. She immediately recognized the invalidity of her husband's criticism.

Generally, people are attracted to their best colors. One day, I was working with a woman who appeared to be in her mid to late thirties. She was attracted to colors that I considered to be wrong for her. The color of her makeup was slightly off, and the color of her clothing was not complimentary to her. After several minutes, she confided in me that she was, in fact, color blind— something very unusual in a woman. I encouraged her to find someone reputable to do a color analysis of her and then always carry her color swatches in her purse. That way, when she was shopping, she could explain to the sales person that she had a problem and needed help selecting these colors. I explained to her that she was far too young and too attractive to go through life wearing colors that were not flattering to her. You only have one opportunity to make a first impression!

Recently, I had cataracts removed from both of my eyes. As cataracts have the tendency to grow very slowly, I experienced firsthand how easily one can grow accustomed to vision that is far from perfect. My first clue came when I would describe the color of a dress to Terrie and she would look puzzled. "Mom, I hate to tell you this, but you are not seeing that color correctly. It must be your cataracts." And here I considered myself a color specialist!! When driving home at night became increasingly difficult, I decided it was time to do something about it.

The morning after the first surgery, when the pirate-like eye shield was removed I was astounded! Everything looked more vivid. Blacks looked darker, reds brighter, greens more intense! How could I have gone as long as I did, putting up with imperfect vision?! When I walked into my store for the first time after surgery, I was amazed at all the beautiful colors. I felt as though I was going into visual overload.

There had been times through the years, before my cataracts began developing, that I had reached the conclusion that the customer I was working with was not seeing the color I was seeing. "Do you have cataracts?" I would often ask. Frequently the answer was "yes". Then it became my turn—and how insidious it was! But now, with my cataracts gone, I am able to see things correctly. I bring this up because the majority of our customers are middle aged, a time in our lives when many of us begin to develop cataracts. I've come to realize that many of these ladies do not realize, just as I did not, what they are missing.

When the surgery on the second eye was completed and I returned to be checked the following day, I was again astounded at what I was able to see when the eye shield was removed. The "fuzziness" in the second eye was gone and, suddenly, I had incredible depth perception. Driving the fifty miles home from Dr. Coffman's office in Bryan, Texas, the bluebonnets and Indian paintbrush wild flowers were in full bloom, and what a visual feast it was! I hope my newfound vision will never become "ordinary" and that I will never cease to be amazed at the beauty of color and the beauty of nature.

In discussing the color distortion caused by cataracts, Dr. Coffman explained that, apart from the other ways in which they distort our vision, cataracts block out to a greater degree the shorter wavelengths such as those in the blue region of the light spectrum. These colors are filtered out even more as the cataracts progress and the result is that color perception is degraded significantly. This is why we sometimes see older women with blue hair. These are women who use a rinse to color their hair. Dr. Coffman said that, to these women with advanced cataracts, their blue hair actually looks yellow!

Having worn glasses since I was twelve years old, I find that now I only have to wear reading glasses occasionally. In expressing my gratitude to Dr. Coffman and his staff at the Texas Regional Eye Center in Bryan, I volunteered that I have had more discomfort having my teeth cleaned at the dentist than I experienced with my cataract surgery! Please, ladies, do yourself a huge favor and have your eyes checked for cataracts. And, if you need cataract surgery, be sure you get a skilled doctor to do it. This is not the time for the amateur hour. After the surgery you will feel as I felt—why did I wait so long? You will enjoy the wedding so much more if you can see everything much more clearly and in true colors!

It is amazing to me how much the color black is a "security blanket" for so many women. In general, it has been my experience that black is an aging color for most women to wear. Royal blue, on the other hand, is just as slimming but actually makes the face look brighter and younger. It's like getting a facelift!

Sometimes, brides will tell me they're having an "all black wedding" and they want the mothers to wear black. I explain to them exactly what black does. It accentuates lines in the face, pulls out dark circles under the eyes, and adds ten to fifteen years to the person's facial features. This is especially true of photographs of anyone over thirty. Since I have never yet had a woman tell me she wants to look older, I advise against being photographed in black. In my opinion, the only ones who can successfully wear solid black are women who have ivory, porcelain-like skin, jet-black hair and whose skin is devoid of wrinkles. Less than *one* percent of the women I have worked with have been able to wear solid black and look good.

I've become such a "color nut" that I cannot watch the national news, talk shows, etc., and not analyze the colors the women are wearing. I am often totally blown away by the color the women wear on television. Do these women not see what *I* see? How can they think they look good when they wear colors that are the same as their hair or skin creating a nondescript, monochromatic look?

I always thought the women on the Fox News Channel were the best-looking women in television news. They also have, in my opinion, the finest makeup artist in the television industry. With rare exceptions, their female newscasters always used to wear the most flattering colors. To my disappointment, some of their blonde female newscasters then began wearing mostly solid black. The contrast between how they look in turquoise, and in royal blue, bright green, bright red, fuchsia, etc. and how they look in black is astounding. Am I the only one who sees this? Solid black is incredibly aging to the face when being photographed.

My father was a great one for puns. He loved puns. He always contended that the only people who agreed with the timeworn statement, "Puns are the lowest form of humor," were those people who couldn't think up puns themselves! Being a minister, he never told jokes that were even remotely off-color, and he certainly never told jokes that contained swear words. Nevertheless, I think this pun was original with him. Telling this joke was as border line as he ever got: One woman says to another woman, "You look like Helen Black." To which the second woman indignantly replies, "You don't look so good in black yourself!" Forty years ago, when my father used to tell this joke, I wasn't in the fashion business and gave it no further thought. I have since come to wonder if my dad ever realized just how close he had gotten to the truth. The fact of the matter is, just about *every* woman *does* look like Helen Black—if you get my point!

When we attend receptions for business people in the bridal industry, Terrie and I are frequently sought out by photographers and told that they can always tell if we have helped the mothers choose their dresses. "They always look the best and photograph the best!" is the reccurring statement. We are pleased when these professionals are so complimentary. "It's definitely worth all the effort it takes to make our mothers look their best!" Terrie and I reaffirm to each other whenever we receive this type of compliment.

One of the most touching follow-up "thank you" calls we've ever received was from a woman who indicated to one of our consultants, that she had never been told that she was pretty. "Five people at the wedding told me I was pretty. No one ever told me that before. Thank you!"

It is words like these that give us our greatest sense of purpose. We want *every one* of our customers to be beautiful and look her best!

When I see a customer in our store trying on a color that does not look good on her, I can't keep quiet. I want every woman to look incredible at her child's wedding. Looking incredible begins with wearing one of your best colors. The goal is *not* to be told your *dress* is incredible, the goal is to be told *you* look incredible! There **is** a difference. When a customer looks best in a less expensive dress, I always encourage her to buy it. This continues to surprise customers when they realize I own the shop. Obviously, we have to sell our dresses to stay in business. But our primary goal has never been, nor will it ever be, to sell a woman the most expensive dress that we can convince her to buy–or perhaps, just as bad, just sell her a dress. Our goal, instead, has always been and will always be to make each woman look her best. If each of our customers looks her best, the sales will naturally follow. We choose our merchandise carefully. Everything in our store sells.

Recently, I was exploring the possibility of expanding our advertising to include a billboard. After getting a quote of almost $4,000 a month, I began to rethink this option. Then it hit me! My *mothers* are my billboards. Each year, thousands of these women walk down the aisle wearing one of our dresses. *They* are our best advertisements!

Customers will sometimes tell us that they have brought a friend along because they know she will be honest. We try not to be insulted. But we let them know, in no uncertain terms, that we will be incredibly honest, because our customers are our walking billboards. It is *our* reputation that is at stake. And we don't do it just for reputation sake: it is also one of the principles by which we live our private lives.

Chapter 10

Selecting Your Dress

Let's face it. Unless you've had a bunch of kids, most of whom have already gotten married, you are venturing into unfamiliar territory. And to make matters even scarier, there doesn't seem to be a lack of advice from one or more well-meaning friends known in the industry as the KIAF (Know It All Friend) and others posing as "experienced." The KIAF can be your worst enemy–not intentionally, perhaps, but your worst enemy nonetheless. Sometimes, but not always in the beginning, they exhibit two characteristics that spell danger: assertiveness and a professed knowledge of fashion which, you might find out too late, they do not possess. This was one of the reasons I felt compelled to write this book. I had heard so many things that didn't make any sense, usually from people who'd attended three weddings making them, in their own eyes, "experts." Three weddings *do not* make *any* person an expert! Having sat on the organ bench so many times, and having been in this business for so many years, I've seen "the good, the bad, and the ugly"!

The most important thing in choosing your dress is finding something in which you feel beautiful! This *does not* mean buying the most expensive dress. It means finding your *very best color* in a *flattering style*. Remember, as a wise person in the fashion industry once said, "What's 'in fashion' is what looks best on *your* body."

Through the years while working with women I have come to believe that there are three areas of comfort to be considered when helping a mother find her dress. I have listed them in what I consider to be the order of importance:

- First and foremost is what I call her *emotional comfort level*

   Does she feel pretty in the dress? Does she like the way she looks in the dress? Is it becoming? If the customer does not feel emotionally comfortable in the dress, then we must find one in which she does.

- Second is her *financial comfort level*

   Does the price of the dress fit within her budget? We always ask a customer if she has established a budget for her dress. We do this not because we want to sell her the most expensive dress possible but to keep from showing her dresses she might fall in love with but might feel she cannot afford. We do not want to add financial stress to anyone's life.

- Third is her *physical comfort level*

   As women, we've grown accustomed to wearing all sorts of uncomfortable undergarments in an attempt to look slimmer and more fashionable. We've come to accept a certain degree of discomfort. However, a customer who chooses a dress that is too small will not only look larger than she would in the right size dress, but will be uncomfortable during the entire wedding celebration. For these reasons, if a dress is even slightly small, we always advise the next larger size even if it means that it will require alterations.

This reminds me that mothers often request a shorter-sleeved dress "because I am so hot-natured at this time of life." It is my opinion that clothing covering the shoulders and upper body has a much greater effect on one's perception of one's body temperature than does a few extra inches of material on the lower part of the forearm. Therefore, I believe that women should not put too much emphasis on this aspect of the dress.

Since we've just discussed the customer's financial comfort level this seems like a good place to talk about the cost of women's clothing. I'm often asked, "Why is women's clothing so expensive, especially when compared to men's clothing?"

First, there are so many sizes as shown in Chapter 4. Then there is the extremely varied range of fabrics and patterns that are used, and perhaps most important of all is the ever-present requirement to come up with new styles. If your husband goes to a social function and a dozen men wear tuxedos that are identical to his, no one thinks anything of it. As a matter of fact its proof *positive* that he is very much "in style." However, if you and another woman go to the same function wearing the exact same dress in the exact fabric and especially in the same color, it's considered a social disaster! (Even so, this happened to Laura Bush as First Lady of the United States. At one White House social function, *three* other women showed up wearing the identical $8500 Oscar de la Renta gown in the identical color—red—that she was wearing.) Women's clothing is always manufactured in smaller quantities, and designers are constantly working *full time* to come up with new styles and new fabrics. There is the ever-constant requirement for each woman to be unique.

Think about the automobile industry. Suppose it had to redesign and retool every three months to produce new and different automobiles. How much more would a car cost compared to its price when body styles remain essentially unchanged for three or four years, as they do now? And this continual "redesigning and re-tooling" does not just apply to dresses and gowns. It applies to shoes, purses, sportswear and almost everything that we women wear!

Compared to women's clothing, men's wear is far more standardized. Those who can remember the late 1950's will recall that, at the end of the decade, three-button suit jackets were the firmly established style. When President Kennedy came into office in 1961 and started wearing two-button jackets, the three button suits were out! The two-button suit was ushered in overnight and remained the style in men's wear not just for years, but for *decades*! Except for relatively minor changes in the width of the lapel, the style almost never varied.

I'm willing to bet that your husband continued to wear the same suits year in and year out and ultimately got rid of them because he wore them out, because they became too small or too large as his weight changed, or because he just got sick and tired of them. As for fabrics and patterns–there is almost no variation in men's fabrics, year after year, and decade after decade. And as regards men's formal wear, if it still fits, the tuxedo your husband wore thirty years ago is still very much in style today.

Women's dresses are another matter. In the final analysis, the relatively high cost of women's clothing is really caused by the norms of our society that place the artificial limitations on how we women are supposed to dress. For some reason, our society dictates that we women must always have something new and different and, inevitably, this costs more!

While we're talking about the price of the mother's dress, there is one aspect of this subject that needs to be addressed, even though I dislike having to discuss it, for fear someone might think I'm pushing more expensive dresses.

Less expensive dresses are manufactured and sold in larger quantities. Department stores all over the country usually place an upper limit on the price of items they carry. The less expensive the dress, the more likely it is to be sold in department stores. This means, therefore, that if you buy one of these dresses, you can have a guest show up at the wedding wearing the same dress that you have chosen.

Believe me, as the daughter of missionaries, I believe that there are bigger issues in life than this. Nevertheless, I have worked with mothers who consider this to be a major problem. One mother told us about her experience as a guest at a wedding. To her dismay, she found that she was wearing an identical dress to that of one of the mothers. She was extremely embarrassed and uncomfortable during the wedding and throughout the entire reception, and stayed as far away from that mother as possible. When choosing your dress, consider whether it may be sold in department stores. If this is not a problem for you, that's fine. However, if it is a concern, you may want to discuss it further with your salesperson.

Through the years I have noticed how a woman's body language will respond when she finds the perfect dress. Very often, she will do a little twirl. Sashay, almost.

Immediately, upon trying on a dress, quite often a customer will say, "This just isn't me." However, the longer she stays in the dress, the more it becomes her. More times than I care to recount, the friend (the KIAF), who has been brought along for moral support and advice, will be the one who first says, "It doesn't look like you." "But it *should*!" is my customary retort.

Often, it takes an experienced salesperson to "lead" you into a better look and frequently out of your old comfort zone. I wish I had a dollar for every customer who has said, after the wedding, "I never would have chosen that dress, but I've never received so many compliments in my life!"

Because a salesperson doesn't know you personally, she can often make a better suggestion as to what will look best on you. She does not have any preconceived notions of how you normally look and what you normally wear. This is why I often find it difficult to work with personal friends of mine. When one comes into the store, I usually get one of the staff to work with her.

Perhaps I need to qualify my definition of a "salesperson" at this point. I am absolutely *not* referring to someone who is *commission driven,* nor am I referring to a cash register operator. I am referring to someone who is trained and highly experienced and has the customer's best interest at heart—someone who is truly attempting to help the customer look her best. This is why we prefer to call our employees "consultants," instead of "sales people." They are there to consult with the customer, find out her special needs, advise her in regard to her special occasion and help the customer look her best. Ringing up the sale on the cash register is the least of what they do.

We pay our staff the same, whether they sell anything or not. We believe that this is best for the customer. We also believe that what is best for the customer is, ultimately, best for us. Because our staff are not paid commissions on their sales, each customer can be assured that she will not be pressured into purchasing a dress that she does not want, nor one that is beyond her budget. Since we do not accept returns, we want every customer to be happy with her purchase when she leaves our store. Only with happy customers is it possible to have the word-of-mouth advertising that we have enjoyed since our store opened in 1991. It is the only type of advertising that is universally believed. It cannot be purchased. It can only be earned. It is priceless.

Where do you go to find a dress for such an important occasion as your child's wedding? Referrals are your best source. If you have been to a wedding where you thought the mother looked outstanding, ask her where she purchased her dress. And be sure you ask her if the sales person was helpful in selecting her dress. Before we even say "hello" to each of our customers, we have already analyzed her coloring and figure. Because we know our inventory intimately, we know, with certainty, which colors and styles of our dresses will look best on her. Try to find a store that can give you this same kind of help.

Sometimes I will ask Terrie, "What is such and such a customer looking for?" and often her immediate response is, "Something that doesn't exist!" For years, the mother (almost never the father!) has been looking forward to her daughter's wedding. She thinks of the joy of seeing relatives and friends. It's the chance to improve on her own wedding and relive it vicariously through her daughter. During this time, she has also been fantasizing about the dress she will wear and even its style and color. But no one makes a dress like that! And certainly not in that size! And, most likely, not in that color! What should she do? Instead of embarking on a quest for something that doesn't exist, she can have the dress of her dreams made, with all the risks and pitfalls that that involves. (See Chapter 11) Or, she could go to a store with competent sales people who can give her good advice and help her find something in which she looks fabulous. I think this is, by far, the better option.

Many things go into the making of a good salesperson or consultant. She becomes one by working with women all day long, thereby gaining the experience to know what will look good on different figures and what won't. She must have a sense of style and an eye for color and she must be extremely familiar with the inventory in the store. She needs to be familiar with what actually takes place during a wedding, what pictures are actually taken, and what is truly important. This is why I have found that hiring mature women, with years of retail clothing experience, has worked better for my store than hiring very young and inexperienced women.

Flowers are an integral part of a wedding and can also have a profound visual effect by choice and placement.

- Corsages for mothers are largely symbolic. Most formal dresses do not need to be further enhanced. In fact, very often a corsage pinned on a dress will actually detract from the lines of the dress rather than add to its attractiveness.

- If a corsage is worn on the dress, it should be worn high on the shoulder. When pinning the corsage to the dress, the shoulder seam provides a reinforced area with less chance of damaging the fabric of the dress. I believe the practice of wearing the corsage lower on the chest was started by people assuming that because a man's boutonniere is placed on his lapel, a woman's corsage should be placed in that area also. If a corsage is placed at chest level, the overall effect is to make the bust seem to sag. However, if the corsage is high up on the shoulder, it actually creates a lift of the bust and draws the eye up to the face creating a much more flattering look.

- An alternative to pinning the corsage on the dress is to carry a purse made of a soft enough material to which the corsage can be pinned. As the mother walks down the aisle, she carries the purse in the crook of her arm similar to the way a football player carries a football. When being photographed, she stands at a 45-degree angle to the camera with her purse held closely just below the waist. During the reception, she simply lays her purse down and gets on with enjoying the festivities.

- Wrist corsages are something I rarely recommend. A "clump" of flowers placed on the wrist tend to flag an area of the body not usually our best feature at this stage of life. The only time I recommend a wrist corsage is when the woman is in a wheelchair or using a walker or a cane or any other ambulatory device. This will draw attention away from the assistive device.

- An additional option is for the mother to carry a single flower or a tussy mussy bouquet down the aisle. It is important to remember that if either of these is chosen, it needs to be in proportion to the size of the mother carrying it. A larger woman carrying a small flower or tiny bouquet will appear to be even larger than she actually is. A larger woman should carry, for example, a canna lily instead of a single rose. (A single rose can look like a blade of grass in extreme cases!)

- It is important to remember that the two mothers' flowers do not have to be identical or even match. One mother may have chosen a plain dress where a corsage would actually add something to the dress. The other may have chosen a more ornate dress where a flower will actually detract from the lines of the dress. One mother may be in a wheelchair or a walker and therefore need a wrist corsage. The final decision about the color and style of the flowers chosen for the mothers is actually made *after* the mothers have chosen their dresses.

- Although the entire flower package for the wedding is normally booked with the florist months in advance, the specifics of the mothers' flowers can be finalized three to four weeks before the wedding. This is another reason for selecting your dress early: so that the flowers chosen can enhance both the style and the color of your dress.

- In situations where a mother is walking the bride down the aisle, I recommend that she not wear or carry any flowers. As she escorts the bride, it is better to have the bride's bouquet as the focal point. The mother's flowers, whether a single flower, tussy mussy, or a corsage pinned on a purse can be placed on the pew where she will be seated. By so doing she will have her flowers for the pictures if she so chooses.

In selecting your dress, here are some of the things you should consider:

- For women who are short, a full-length dress will create a taller, thinner look. It is also true for a plus-size woman. This is why most women look taller and thinner when wearing long pants.

- No matter the size of the woman, a dress with a jacket the same length as that of the skirt tends to make a woman look like a refrigerator—a rectangle—albeit a small refrigerator or a large refrigerator. For a more flattering look, the jacket needs to be longer than the skirt or the skirt needs to be longer than the jacket.

- To avoid looking larger than you are, be sure the garment is not hugging you in any of your "problem" areas. Fabric skimming over your body will create a slimmer look.

- Forget about the little numbers sewn in the back of the dress! No one else will see them. Concentrate on the dress that looks the best on you, *not* the size shown on the label.

- A well-fitting garment will actually make a woman look smaller. Producing the bride or groom has done a number on most of our figures. Therefore, it is unrealistic at this time in life for a woman to expect to get away with no alterations. A few women do, but by far, they are the exception rather than the rule.

- "Free alterations" are *never* free. Think about it. People must get paid for their labor. If alterations are included in the price of the dress, then the price of every dress must include enough to cover the cost of alterations—needed or not! With so-called "free alterations" you are almost certainly paying for alterations you do not need!

- Mothers confined to wheelchairs should wear dresses long enough to at least cover their calves. Many women will choose to wear a dressy pantsuit. If choosing to wear a long dress, the sides of the dress can be bustled to avoid getting the skirt entangled in the wheels. Where the side seams of the dress intersect the hem, small buttons can be attached, and the dress bustled to inconspicuous loops sewn on either side of the waist. This minor alteration allows the mother's legs to be fully covered and keeps the sides of the dress out of the wheels. I have recommended this for years and it solves a problem for those who need to use a wheelchair.

- A V-neck will make the torso look longer, thereby giving a taller, thinner look.

- If your hips are as wide as your shoulders, an off-the-shoulder neckline should *not* be worn. This style creates two equal horizontal lines, which then create a shorter, heavier look.

- Shoulder pads can create a 15 pounds lighter look! I recommend the "wedge" type shoulder pad with the thin edge nearest the neck, and the thick edge where the sleeve is sewn to the dress. These can be worn under the bra straps. I do **not** recommend shoulder pads that are rounded in the area where the sleeve is attached to the dress. This is the shape we are trying *to correct*. As we grow older, we tend to round down in the shoulder area. As a consequence, this leaves clothes ill fitting and also causes the bust to appear to sag down. The correct type of shoulder pads which are added to straighten the shoulder "slope" can give the illusion of lifting the bust area and actually bringing in the hips. (Eighty-five percent of the time, I recommend adding shoulder pads to pads that are already in the garment.).

Some women believe that shoulder pads are old fashioned and, therefore, out of style. Nothing could be further from the truth! Some women even brag that when they buy a new dress, the first thing they do is remove the shoulder pads because they're out-dated. For goodness sake, don't do this!–unless they are the rounded type described previously. Using the proper type of shoulder pads will square up your shoulders, without making you look like a football player suited up for the game.

With proper padding in the shoulders you can instantly appear to be slimmer.

Shoulder pads are often available in lingerie departments and in fabric stores.

- Extending the edge of the shoulder can actually make the hips appear smaller, creating a better and a more slimming silhouette. Think of a triangle. As far as the female figure is concerned, a triangle pointing down is more flattering than a triangle that is pointing up.

- For women with large arms extending well beyond the edge of their shoulders, shoulder pads will help to create a slimmer illusion.

- Women who are very tall often have difficulty finding a dress long enough to be "full length." Experienced salespeople can direct you towards designers who make longer dresses. One of our sources for longer dresses has a female executive who is over 6 ft. tall. She has been able to impact her company's decision to make extra-long dresses.

- Very tall women would be wise to stay away from ankle length dresses, as they tend to make it look as though they've "outgrown" the dress. That length is neither "fish nor fowl." Mid-calf or to-the-floor are better choices!

- As a point of interest, if a woman wears a belt, the belt should bear some proportionality to the size of the wearer. A large woman wearing a narrow belt makes the woman look larger than she is.

- If a woman is going to wear jewelry, it should bear some proportionality to her size. For example, a large person who wears a small broach, small earrings or a small necklace will look even larger.

I remember the customer who came to the store looking for a skirt in one color and a top in another to wear to her child's wedding. The problem with this request was that she was really short and very heavy. Trying to ease her into something that would be more complimentary to her height and shape, I brought her an outfit in a solid color. Her tall, extremely thin husband immediately rejected my suggestion without her even trying it on. He volunteered that he was used to seeing her in two-piece, two-color outfits. I tactfully explained that a solid color would actually make her appear taller and thinner.

Apparently, the "familiar look" fell into their "comfort zone," even though it was, by no means, her best look. The type of thing they were looking for, especially in her size, was not something I chose to carry in the store. It was apparent that *he* was going to decide what she looked best in. Her opinion and ours did not matter. Although I could have offered to order it, I chose not to do so. I realized that, once again, the price of honesty is sometimes no sale. But I thought to myself that, at least, she would not be able to tell others who saw her at the wedding that she had bought her dress at T. Carolyn. Bill Cosby was quoted as having said, "I'm not sure what the path to success is, but the path to failure is trying to please everyone."

One Saturday, I was working with four women in front of the big, three-way mirror. A husband, who was there with his wife, sat quietly watching and listening as I worked with each of the women. As I finished with the fourth he remarked, "I will never again look at *any* woman and believe that what I'm seeing is real! All I've heard for the last 30 minutes is 'We do this to create this illusion and we do that to create that illusion.' It's all illusion!"

Isn't it great being women when we can have all these tricks up our sleeves?!

Chapter 11

Maybe I'll Have One Made

If I had a dollar for every woman who has called me on the phone or come into the store telling me they were having or had had something made and have discovered they *hate* it, I would be a very wealthy woman!

It continues to puzzle me that women will opt to have something made from scratch, rather than have alterations to a dress that they have tried on in a store. To me this is like buying a "pig in a poke." Until you try it on, you will not know whether it fits or whether or not you will like it.

I have to be very careful how I respond to "Maybe I'll have something made" because customers could think it is part of a sales pitch. The fact of the matter is this: *Unless* you have tried on a dress of the exact style and know that it is flattering, *and unless* the dress you are having made is of the exact type of fabric as the dress you tried on (you cannot go from chiffon to brocade, for example), and, obviously, *unless* you know that the person making the dress is capable, you can be in store for a traumatic situation. (These are a lot of "*unlesses*"!)

With very few exceptions, "homemade" dresses look "homemade." By the time a dress reaches a store as merchandise, multiple "mock-ups" (prototypes) have been made of that dress prior to production. With each mock-up, the pattern is tweaked to achieve the finished look. The prototype has been tried and fitted on a human body, the model, and adjusted, as many as 15 or more times. When someone is making a dress for you, they are making that *one* dress for the *first* time. It is, in fact, an original prototype that has not been refined. There is no tweaking. Seams are generally much bulkier than a "store-bought" dress, thus giving it that "homemade" appearance. Obviously, there are exceptions to this, but more times than not, the finished product is not professional looking.

I had a customer come to the store one morning on her way to Dallas to attend her son's wedding. She told me that she had had two outfits made "by the finest seamstress in town" and neither fit properly nor looked right. She had spent $1,200 for labor alone! Now she was in my store trying to find something to wear to the wedding 24 hours before the actual event! As she left, two new garments in hand, she was contemplating taking the seamstress to small claims court.

Another lady called asking for directions to our store. When she had gone to try on her dress for the final fitting that morning she discovered that she "looked like a stuffed sausage!"

Years before opening the store, I had my own experience with "maybe I'll have one made."

It was for me to wear to my daughter's first wedding. We were preparing to move back to Alaska on a temporary assignment. Her wedding was to be held on January 2 and we would be in Alaska from the previous August to the following August.

Being a fairly organized person, I had purchased the material for two outfits. One was to be worn at the wedding, and the other for the family reunion to be held the day after the wedding. I delivered the material to the seamstress in July. When I returned to Houston in November for a brief visit, I was concerned that she hadn't started on either garment.

Unbeknownst to me, this lady suffered from depression and spent quite a bit of time curled up in bed in the fetal position! My dress for the wedding was ready at 5 o'clock *the night before the wedding* and my reunion outfit was completed *three weeks after* the event!

Terrie's mother-in-law-to-be, who lived in Kansas, was also having her dress made. The fabric she had chosen was very expensive, delicate silk. Her seamstress made the entire garment with the silk sewn wrong side out! The seams could not be ripped out and re-sewn without damaging the material because it was so fragile. Consequently, she was forced to wear this expensive dress to the wedding with the fabric reversed!

A lady, while buying her dress from us, told us that she was very concerned because the woman who was making the bridesmaids' dresses didn't seem to be up to the task. She called me several times, each time more concerned than before. This worried mother needed a sympathetic listener and someone who could, perhaps, give her some hope or reassurance. Late one evening, as I was working in the back office, the phone rang. It was this mother. She was in an absolute panic. It was, by now, the night before the wedding. The bridesmaids' dresses had just been completed and *not one* of them fit correctly. She was in tears, the bride was in tears, and the bridesmaids were in despair.

I felt so sorry for these people, even though I had absolutely nothing to do with these bridesmaids' dresses. (Remember, we don't even sell bridesmaids' dresses!) The next morning, the first thing I did was to call the little lady down the street to whom we refer alterations. She dropped everything she was doing and miraculously pinned, re-cut, and re-sewed each of the dresses so that the girls were able to wear them that evening! The mother and bride were eternally grateful.

On the Wednesday before a Saturday wedding, a lady came to our store looking for a dress. She told us one of the saddest stories we've ever heard in the category of "maybe I'll have one made."

She had taken the fabric and everything else that was needed to make the dress, to an older seamstress with years of experience and a wonderful reputation. At the first fitting, one dart in the bust area was 3 inches higher than the other. The armholes were uneven, the hem was uneven and the lining did not fit the dress. Because there were so many problems with the dress being made, the customer then took to the seamstress a brand new dress which she had just purchased and which fit perfectly, hoping she could take the measurements from this dress and thereby salvage the dress that was being made.

At the next fitting she discovered that, the seamstress had, by then, made the dress 4 inches smaller and admitted that she had no explanation for why she had done so. Furthermore, she had marked the fabric with a red ballpoint pen where the darts were supposed to be, leaving permanent ink marks on the right side of the fabric. Additionally, the dress that was only to have been used as a template had been altered and *it* too was now unwearable, although she could not explain why she had done this. A brand new jacket that the customer had taken in for minor alterations by this seamstress ended up with the sleeves shortened and the armholes made bigger, none of which was supposed to have been touched. It, too, had been ruined. "I guess I'm forgetting more than I'm remembering these days," the poor woman sadly confessed. Our customer found out, too late, that this unfortunate seamstress was now apparently suffering from some form of dementia and could no longer perform the high quality of work for which she had been so well known.

As it turned out, this customer found a dress at our store that she liked better and which was less expensive than the one this seamstress was supposed to have made.

Remember, if you are determined to have something made, *be sure* you have tried on that *exact style* in *exactly the same type of fabric. Be sure* that the person making your dress really *knows* what he or she is doing and will make a professional looking garment for you. And, most important of all, *be sure* that the person making the dress has *plenty of time* to do it, so that if it doesn't look right you will have enough time to search for an alternative. This is **not** the time for the "homemade" look. I am sure there are many competent seamstresses, but this has been my experience over the past 18 years.

Chapter 12

Returns, Rentals, and the Internet

Returns

A few months after we opened the store in 1991, "The Wall Street Journal" had an article on its inside pages discussing the practice of customers purchasing formal wear, wearing the garments and then returning them for a refund. I have always regretted not saving that article and having it framed and hanging it in our store. A year or two later, Oprah Winfrey devoted one of her hour-long shows to the practice. Women spoke shamelessly of buying expensive clothes, wearing them and returning them for a full refund, and stated that they had no qualms of conscience about doing so. When newspaper articles and entire television programs have been centered on women bragging about wearing and then returning formal wear, you begin to understand the depth of this problem.

Several weeks after Terrie and I opened T. Carolyn a woman in the neighborhood brought back the dress she had bought from us. She was one of our first customers. She told us the sad story that the wedding had been cancelled. She realized she could never wear the dress because of the painful memories it would evoke—in fact she couldn't even bear to look at it hanging in her closet. Could she please return it? This was the first time we had encountered this. She seemed so sincere. We believed *everything* she said (honest people are often the most gullible), sympathized with her, refunded her every penny she had paid us for the dress, and put the dress back on the rack. This was our first "return."

The very next customer who tried it on exclaimed that there were food stains on the dress! Upon closer examination, it was apparent the dress had, indeed, been worn. In fact, the cleaners informed us that the dress had already been dry cleaned not once, but several times! It was at this point that we were forced to institute an "All Sales Final" policy. We discarded the dress and considered it the price of tuition.

Customers should realize that when they shop at a store with an "all sales final" policy, they are guaranteed that their purchase has never been worn before, perspired in, hung in a smoker's closet, been around cat or dog dander, or subject to intense heat while stored or hung in someone's car.

"All sales final" is not a friend of the indecisive, the insecure, or the customer who intends to wear it and then return it.

I'm asked frequently, "But what if it still has the tags on?" With tagging guns being easily accessible to the public, tags that are still on the garment guarantee nothing. But many don't go to the extent of buying a tagging gun. I had an interesting conversation with an executive of a dry cleaning chain. "You'd never believe how many women bring things in to be cleaned, requesting that we not damage the tags that are still attached to the garments," he said.

The problem of returns has been fueled by some of the larger chain stores in the past having a policy of taking back anything, anytime.

One evening I was browsing through the formal wear racks in a department store, just to see what they had. I struck up a conversation with the department manager who happened to be on the floor. We began discussing the problems with "returns" and she said something quite interesting, "I never buy a little black dress off the rack because I know, that by the time I purchase it, that dress will have gone to at least four parties I didn't attend!"

One of my first employees had previously worked at a large department store in Houston. The day after New Year's Day, a woman came into the department store to return a dress and jewelry. Our employee immediately recognized this woman. They both had attended the same New Year's Eve party. The woman was returning the same dress and costume jewelry she had worn to the party they had both attended. The store's policy was to accept returns.

A current member of my staff worked for a large family-owned clothing store in another state. At this store, she had witnessed things being brought back, tattered, dirty, and smelling of tobacco smoke and very obviously having been worn. Some even had to be discarded. This store, which had been started by the patriarch of the family and was then being run by his son, ultimately went out of business.

As a family owned boutique, compared to a department store, we would never be able to control our inventory if customers were allowed to keep things and return them. I previously referred to the mother of the groom who told us the other mother had five outfits in her closet. She intended to decide the morning of the wedding which one she would wear and would return the others after the wedding!

The grisliest story we ever heard about returns came from another storeowner at a seminar Terrie and I were attending. Three days after purchasing a dress, the customer returned it. The storeowner retagged it and put it back on the rack. The next person who bought the dress brought it back complaining that it caused her to breakout in a terrible rash and the longer she wore it the more ill she became.

The situation escalated, and the storeowner's insurance company eventually got involved. Chemical testing disclosed that the dress was contaminated with *embalming fluid* causing the second purchaser of the dress to have a severe reaction. Although the original purchaser admitted nothing, it does not take a lot of imagination to think of the possible ways whereby this garment could have become contaminated, especially in the hands of an unscrupulous customer. Eventually the insurance company settled with the lady for a significant sum of money. Our policy of "all sales final" protects not just us, but the customer as well.

One of the sales reps in one of the showrooms at the Apparel Mart told me, that before becoming a sales rep, he had owned an upscale boutique in Houston. He had been forced to close this boutique because of returns. As an example, one of his customers had purchased a gown that was over $2,500 to be worn at a function here in Houston, where a member of the British Royal Family was being honored.

The day after the reception, this customer, the wife of a foreign government official assigned to Houston, was pictured in the Houston Chronicle along side the visiting member of the Royal Family. She was wearing the gown she had purchased in his boutique. A few days later she came into his store to return the gown, claiming that she'd never worn it. He confronted her with the picture and refused to return her money. Upon being refused, she became enraged and threw the gown at him. She followed up with a request for a chargeback on her credit card in a letter to the credit card company written on embassy stationary. Even though the owner had absolute proof that she had worn the gown, the credit card company rewarded her bad behavior and refunded her money. Unfortunately, that was quite common several years ago. Nowadays, the credit card companies realize the importance of backing retailers when such absurd and dishonest chargeback claims are made.

Rentals

Occasionally, I'll get a phone call from someone asking if we rent ladies formal wear. Obviously, we don't.

At the time you make arrangements to rent a garment, you have no guarantee what condition it is going to be in by the time *your* turn comes around. You also have no idea *where* that garment has been and *who* has been wearing it.

The problem with renting women's formal wear is that it is unlikely the garments have been dry cleaned after *every* use. Some of the fabrics are too delicate to be dry cleaned after each wearing. Several different people may very well have worn a rented garment before it is cleaned again. To me, this is as bad or worse than sleeping on a stranger's sheets that haven't been washed!

I have read articles written by dermatologists about skin infections that can be caught from wearing rented clothing. Borrowing a dress from a family member or a close friend is one thing. Wearing something worn for hours by strangers is quite another.

The Internet

With the advent of the Internet, things are changing in the retail business and not always for the best. Unfortunately, in this day and age, many people are using bridal stores strictly to try things on. Stores are complaining bitterly about brides who take up hours of their time, only to order from the Internet instead, thinking they can save a few dollars. These customers have no intention of purchasing from the store or boutique. They have no conscience about taking up the time of the employees, seeking their professional advice as to color and style, drinking their coffee, and "sucking up" their heating and air conditioning! If this continues, there will be fewer and fewer stores for these customers to use for the purpose of trying clothes on. As a result, many stores are demanding that manufacturers not sell to Internet sellers who do not have an actual store, a "brick and mortar" store, as we call it in the industry.

Increasingly, brides seem more tempted to buy their gowns on the Internet—often with disastrous results. Brides don't understand that, in the end, they are often paying more for gowns that they buy on the Internet— even if they are fortunate enough to get a first-quality gown. A store normally includes steaming with the purchase of the gown. When a gown is bought on the Internet, the bride will have to pay someone to steam it. She will also find that alterations are often more expensive than in-house alterations by a bridal store.

For a seller to be able to carry a line of merchandise, a manufacturer requires the seller to purchase a significant number of pieces. Many Internet sellers are not authorized to sell the line and have no inventory. A lot of the Internet sellers are actually selling out of a room in their house. They are depending on a less than scrupulous small store, usually in another city or even in another state, to get the merchandise for them. Once the manufacturer gets wind of this, they can refuse to ship any more merchandise to the store, thereby leaving the Internet seller without access to the merchandise and leaving the bride with no gown.

I cannot tell you how many horror stories I've heard of incorrectly sized gowns, dirty gowns, even tattered gowns and gowns of the wrong style arriving with the bride having no recourse. Phone calls go unreturned and the bride is stuck! As I've said, we do not sell bridal gowns but this is my "free advice" to brides.

I received a call one day from a lady who had shopped in my store. I had worked with her for a couple of hours and helped her find the "perfect" dress. She had figure problems and the dress I suggested hid these nicely. She left the store saying she would return within the next couple of days to purchase it.

I heard nothing more from her until this phone call. It turned out her son had convinced her that she could find a "better deal" on the Internet. She took his advice and purchased the identical dress sight unseen. When the dress arrived, it was the wrong size. Repeated phone calls to the seller went unanswered and now she was facing major, expensive alterations. In the end, the dress cost her considerably more than it would have had she purchased it in my store.

Unfortunately, there are many unscrupulous websites, which appear to be legitimate businesses. Many of these are actually originating in China. The beautiful pictures of the gowns they feature on their sites have been "lifted" from major designers' sites, obviously without permission. They seduce the bride and her mother into thinking they can have a "copy" of these gowns at a fraction of the cost of purchasing the garment in a real store. When the garment arrives weeks or months later, they are horrified to find that the garment they have received is either a shoddily made copy or looks nothing like the picture they saw on the website. At this point they have no other choice than to go out and try to find something off the rack. This can present a huge problem depending on the time remaining, the size and the color. Often it is impossible to retrieve the money that was spent on this counterfeit garment. I know of one manufacturer who has spent hundreds of thousands of dollars policing the web and hiring attorneys to protect his company's designs from these counterfeiters and interlopers.

Websites originating in China are not the only problem. Websites for businesses located in the United States must also be treated with caution. Garments purchased on these websites may have defects or may be damaged, and your avenues of recourse may be limited. Personally, I never buy *anything* on the Internet unless I know that the seller is reputable.

Don't think that every dress that leaves the factory is perfect. You would probably be surprised if you knew how many garments we have had to return to the vendors over the years. These number in the hundreds and probably in the thousands. Occasionally, we receive garments marred with small spots of sewing machine oil. Some have ink marks or even small ink dots that have been inadvertently deposited on the fabric while tracing the pattern. Stains often cannot be removed without leaving a mark caused by the cleaning fluid itself. Some dresses come to us with fabric defects, some of which are so subtle they can only be seen when viewed at a particular angle or when seen under certain lighting conditions. Still, others are far more obvious. Occasionally, we will receive a two-piece garment in which the two pieces are a very slightly different shade of the same color—just enough to look like a mismatch. Sometimes the hem is uneven or puckered. Sometimes, there is a problem with a seam. Sometimes, the zipper is improperly sewn into the garment.

It has been our experience that with some manufacturers we have very few defective pieces, but with others, defective merchandise is almost the norm. Because of this, we have to have an employee whose main job is to inspect every garment as soon as we receive it. Obviously, this adds to our overhead expenses but it ensures that the customer receives a garment free of defects.

Nowadays, with more and more competition to produce less expensive garments, defects in merchandise from some manufacturers are far more commonplace than they were in the past. Before we put a garment out on the floor, we rigorously inspect it. We have to do this as soon as we receive it, because vendors only allow a very short period for returns. When you buy on the Internet, you need to be certain that the garment you are buying has gone through the same kind of rigorous inspection.

A few years after we opened our store, someone opened a ladies' formal wear store less than two miles from our shop. This store was, at least, four times the size of ours. According to his newspaper advertisements, the owner had stores in Dallas and Houston and others were "opening soon" in Atlanta and other major cities. At the time his store opened here in Houston, one of the sales reps who called on us and who evidently had the inside scoop, told us that it was this person's intention to open many stores quickly, sell them, and make his money in five years and retire. We didn't know whether to believe this or not, and decided to check out his operation.

What we found surprised us. Most, if not all, of his merchandise were samples, seconds, and merchandise purchased from stores going out of business, many with significant damage or defects. The price of virtually every one of these garments was marked up and then marked back down. The price then was the same or higher than it would have been if it were an identical first quality garment in our store. The shop that did most of the alterations for this store's customers told us that virtually every garment had to be repaired to one extent or another.

Just a few years later, his store closed. We were told later that, for quite a long time before he closed his store, this man had stopped paying his vendors and had left them holding the bag when his business shut down. Presumably, he is now retired and enjoying the money he made by less than honorable means.

The purpose of the stories in this and the previous chapter is not to encourage you to buy from no one but us. The purpose, instead, is to urge you to *buy from someone you can trust*. The best way to do this is to make inquiries. If you meet someone who looks beautiful in her gown or dress or suit, ask her where she bought it. Ask her if the sales staff took a personal interest in helping her look her best. Ask if they were sufficiently knowledgeable in women's clothing and women's styles and sufficiently familiar with the dresses they had in stock to help her find what she really needed. Finally, ask her if the sales staff was sufficiently familiar with the etiquette applicable to the event to be able to give her guidance about the proper attire. Buy only from someone whom you feel you can trust.

There are many pitfalls in buying an expensive garment. *Caveat emptor*—buyer beware!

Chapter 13

What's Next?

There's an old saying in the bridal industry, "How does the mother of the bride (or groom) spell "relief?"

O-V-E-R!!

After months and sometimes years of planning, the wedding has finally come and gone. Now what?

My son, who was married for the first time at the age of thirty-five, said something oh, so true. "Mom," he said, "people spend more time planning the wedding than they do the marriage."

Through the years, I've seen brides and mothers fret over the most miniscule thing and spend hours over trivia. Terrie, who has experienced personal tragedy in her life, has often pulled me aside and said, "If they think *this* is a problem, they need to fasten their seat belts for what life may have in store for them!"

Weddings are, in fact, a wonderful occasion. It is a time when most of the people who care about you are gathered under one roof. The only other time this happens is at funerals. But weddings are so much happier!

"What's next?" you ponder, as the bride and groom depart for the honeymoon.

Hopefully, and in due time, grandchildren!! Speaking from personal experience, I can tell you that God gives you grandchildren at a time in your life when everything seems mundane and ordinary. With their arrival, comes the excitement of seeing things through a child's eyes, and life becomes new and exciting again.

A business friend of mine summed it all up when she told me, "It's 'do-over' time." There aren't too many times in life when you have a chance to do something over again. Being a grandparent gives you a chance to do it over again and correct your mistakes this time.

And so, continues the cycle of life.

Chapter 14

In Conclusion

In the second year of business, the husband of one of our designers asked me what I thought contributed to our "success." I must confess I certainly didn't feel very "successful." Cash flow was still an enormous consideration, and had it not been for my husband's faith in our efforts and willingness to dip into our savings, we could never have continued to keep the doors of T. Carolyn open.

People interested in emulating our success, occasionally ask our advice about opening their own business. We truthfully respond that, had we known ahead of time what was involved, we probably would not have had the courage to do it. We ask about their motive. Do they really enjoy helping people—or do they just want to make money? If it is the latter, there must be an easier way to do it! Are they prepared to go years without making a profit and wait ten to fifteen years to establish a reputation? We have found, through our own experience that these things come neither quickly nor easily. And once your reputation is established, you must guard it jealously. This includes always keeping your word, being fair and honest to customers, as well as your vendors, and making sure that your employees always do the same. "A good name is rather to be chosen than great riches ..." (Proverbs 22:1). Once your good reputation is lost, it can never be regained.

Looking back over the past eighteen years, I have come to the conclusion that Terrie's and my decision to do only the things and implement only the procedures that made common sense to us, as women, has been a large factor in our success. A glaring example of this was a conversation we had with the then-president of a local bank. He was attending a luncheon of local business owners, as were we. After the luncheon, while walking to our respective cars, we met briefly in the parking lot. He informed us that we were really brave to start this business, as everyone he knew who had attempted anything like what we were attempting had failed! Then he proceeded to quiz us about certain practices and procedures. When we indicated that we were not implementing any of those practices and procedures, he admonished us that we really should!

As we got into our car, Terrie turned to me and said, "Mom, it must be a 'man thing'. Everyone he knows in this business has failed, and yet, as a man, he feels compelled to advise us women to follow the same flawed procedures."

Perhaps it is because of my background as the daughter of missionaries, but I can honestly say that the greatest feeling of satisfaction that I receive in our business comes from knowing that I have helped someone. A large majority of our customers are in mid-life, a time when many people face severe problems and crises of one form or another. Some have just become, or are about to become divorced. Many of our customers are experiencing significant physical problems of which overweight and difficult-to-fit figures are often the least significant. A significant number of our customers have life-threatening health problems that have affected their physical appearance and sometimes their mobility. Still, others have parents who are terminally ill. Conflicting demands on their time and attention, imposed by their parents' condition and by their child's upcoming wedding, compound the stress that they are under. A few are even terminally ill themselves and must be treated with the greatest understanding and compassion. To one extent or another, all of our customers need help. Some just need good fashion advice. Most of them need someone who can offer reassurance. Many need sympathetic and compassionate understanding and someone who can help them look their best in very difficult situations.

Whenever I see a customer come through the door, my first thought is, "Here is someone who has a problem, perhaps I can help her." I never think, "Here comes someone to whom I can probably sell a dress." I believe that most customers sense that Terrie and I, together with our staff, are genuinely concerned about them as individuals and want them to have what's best for them.

Often on a crowded Saturday, a customer will come to me and say, "Do you work here?" To which I usually reply, "Boy, do I ever!" When they realize that I am, in fact, one of the owners, they often express surprise. For some reason the image of an owner actually being on site and working the floor seems unusual. How else would I be informed as to how garments are actually fitting, which designs work best on which figures, and what most women are asking for? It is my contention that off-site buyers for stores are not always in touch with the real world of retailing, thereby leading to some merchandise-buying blunders.

Customers who live on the other side of Houston often say, "Why don't you have another store nearer to where I live? This is such a long drive!" There are two answers to that question. The first is that, at least half of our customers come from many other parts of Texas, other states and other countries. Many of our customers drive here from Dallas, Austin, San Antonio, and Corpus Christi. They come from the contiguous states of Louisiana, Arkansas, Oklahoma and New Mexico as well as from every other state in the Union. A second store would make little difference to them. But the second and most important reason that we don't have a second store is this: we have never been able to figure out a way to have a second store and give our customers the same level of personal service for which we have become known. By working with us every day, our employees come to realize just how important personal service to the customer is to *us*. Our employees, thereby, come to emulate our concern for the customer. Believe me, if we can ever figure out a way to do it, we *will* have a second store, and perhaps a third and maybe even a fourth!

As I've said, our customers come not only from Houston and all over Texas, but also from all of the other states, including Alaska and Hawaii, as well as from many foreign countries. Even though we have a significant advertising budget and have a well known website, www.tcarolyn.com, we are always eager to know how our customers have heard about us. We conduct surveys from time to time. Each time we find that, despite all the advertisement that we purchase, 90 percent of our customers are referred by other customers. This naturally has produced some interesting stories.

After we'd been in business several years, we were conducting one such survey. One of the ladies we interviewed told us that she was standing in line with a friend waiting to enter a museum in Moscow. They were discussing her daughter's upcoming wedding. She mentioned that she would be going to Houston the following week to see her daughter and plan for the wedding. Suddenly, someone behind her tapped her on the shoulder. She turned to see who it was. This person, whom she had never met, had overheard her conversation and asked, "Have you already got your dress for the wedding?" When she said, "No," this lady then said to her, "When you get to Houston, you absolutely must go to T. Carolyn. They are the best!"

Another customer, who was about to undergo anesthesia prior to surgery in one of the hospitals at the large Houston Medical Center, said to the nurse, "Please don't bruise my arm. My daughter is getting married in two weeks." The nurse asked if she'd bought her dress yet. When she replied, "No," the nurse said, "Go to T. Carolyn. Don't waste your time going anywhere else."

Yet another customer, who bought a dress at our store, told me that she was shopping for a mother's dress in a well-known store in Houston. When she went into the dressing room, unsolicited advice came from a faceless voice in the adjoining cubicle. "Before you buy anything here, you really need to go to T. Carolyn."

Although she never saw this person and never found out who this person was, she took her advice! Believe me, this kind of reputation has to be most carefully protected.

These are the kind of stories that warm our hearts. In the end, they make it all worthwhile. Almost as heartwarming, are the phone calls we receive from women in countries, sometimes on the other side of the world, who are coming to the States in the near future and have been advised to visit our store. Some, quite often, even make a detour through Houston to shop at our store while en route to their final destination.

My approach to advising women has been based on common sense. Obviously, having attended so many weddings as a musician has given me "hands-on, been-there experience" and enabled me to sift through the myriad bits of misinformation. I have tried to bring a common sense approach to what *really* is important at a wedding.

After working with thousands of women through the years, I have come to the conclusion that, due to their lack of self-confidence, some women do not feel comfortable looking their best. This really frustrates me, as our goal has always been to have *every* customer look her best. I was expressing this frustration to Terrie one day. When I finished speaking, she looked at me and said earnestly, "Mom, short of starting a twelve-step program for women who come to our store, I don't know what more we can do!"

In writing this book it has never been my intention to ridicule or make fun of anyone, but rather to share stories, to teach, and to enlighten. In my days as a student and later as a teacher, I have found that the best teachers are those who can use an anecdote to illustrate an important point.

In reading this book, I hope you have been able to identify with other mothers and realize that you are not alone in your concerns and feelings. It is my hope that this book will have given you the encouragement you need to stand up for yourself and stand up for your "rights." Again, remember that **mothers have rights too:**

- The right to be respected,
- The right to look your best, and, above all else,
- The right to **choose your own dress!**

Should a situation arise where you feel you need moral support, you may want to underline a thought or a passage and show it to the bride. Sometimes it may be necessary to show it to both the bride and her mother. Then she or they can come after *me*. *I* can be the "bad guy." My hope is that you will have felt as though you have something in common with some of the other mothers in this book, thereby giving you the necessary encouragement you need to stand up for yourself when it comes to choosing your own dress for the wedding.

You have been given guidelines for choosing the second most important dress you will ever purchase, remembering that your own wedding gown is usually number one. This will be the second most photographed occasion in your life after your own wedding. Always remember that it may be her day, but **YOU** made it all possible and I'm not referring to just financial help, either.

Hang in there, Mom!

From the Manufacturer's and Designer's Point of View

Stephen N. Lang, CEO, Mon Cheri Bridals, LLC

Mon Cheri labels include - Montage, Montage Boutique, Cameron Blake, Rina Di Montella, Tony Bowles, Occasions, and 2Be:

"Mothers of the bride and groom have been neglected by dress manufacturers for years. In 1993 we decided that needed to end. With the launch of our new line, moms finally had dresses that made them look younger rather than older. Gone were the shapeless sacks that stereotyped the typical mother's dress.

"Our designers studied fashion, sizing, fabrics and fabrications, as well as colors in order to make their designs shine and to flatter any customer. In creating the new look, fabrications chosen were more interesting, many purchased from the finest mills in the Orient. Laces had to be exquisite; colors had to be offered in a wide range to cater to any skin tone. Jackets had to be more youthful to compliment the more stylish dresses. For the woman who didn't want a jacket, shawls had to be available. Sizing had to be more generous and not just offered in the standard missy Sizes 4 to 20. There had to be plus-sizes for the fuller figures and woman's petite sizing that offered a better fit for short women who weren't a Size 8! These were all major considerations we had to take in to account when launching our new line in 1993. The same considerations are constantly being reviewed and refined on a daily basis ensuring that our garments continue to be stylish and up to date.

"We are proud of what we do, of the fine retailers that sell our garments, and of course ultimately, the consumers who choose to wear our clothes."

Ursula Garreau, CEO, Ursula of Switzerland, Inc.:

"In Switzerland, I learned the skills that helped me bring my ideas and designs to the United States and in doing so, found that the American women embraced my fashion style. As my fashions evolved from earlier designs to today's look, our customers grew with me from that seventies style to today's softer elegance.

"It pleases me to see the joy my fashions bring to a customer's special day! To this day, Ursula of Switzerland's collections are renowned internationally for their aura of femininity and elegance.

"Our designs are created with the idea of flattering every woman's dream day. Ursula's fashions have a unique aura that is impossible to imitate. It is this vision that has attracted the loyalty of our customers."

Vivian, Design Team
Jasmine Enterprises, Inc.
Jade by Jasmine:

"Designing wedding gowns and mothers' dresses is a pleasant and rewarding process. The most challenging task for me is to create dress patterns that are aimed to fit every kind of body shape. One example is the cup size. At one time we heard that there were complaints from brides about the cup size of our gowns not being large enough. To find a solution, we went out and bought a lot of different sized bras. We measured and studied them in every possible way we could. We also bought a "Playboy" magazine just to see fuller, rounded shaped breasts. To a conservative single girl like me, that was a most memorable and interesting experience!

"A wedding is the prelude to a couple's lifelong journey. I am a proud member of a great design team that creates beautiful gowns to make the bride's wedding day perfect."

Elenitsa Damianou,
DAMIANOU®:

"My vision of the Mother of the Bride is that of effortless elegance and youthful sophistication regardless of age or size.

"I recently received a letter from a grandmother. It said, 'My granddaughter got married in September and my daughter and I both wore Damianou dresses. You make beautiful clothes that fit so well!' She goes on to say that they had many choices to pick from and that they both received many compliments on their outfits. She concludes, 'The dresses were so comfortable to wear. You do a fantastic job. I am enclosing 2 pictures to show you how the dresses looked on us.'

"I felt so touched and proud looking at those pictures, as though they were members of my own family. So from my point of view that's what it's all about."

About the Author

Barbara Coolidge Tibbetts was born the daughter of a minister. At the age of five, when her parents became missionaries, the family, which included four children, moved to Trinidad, (then British West Indies), an island fourteen miles off the coast of Venezuela.

The missionary board, not wanting the children's education to suffer, agreed to have Barbara, her sister Mary and brother David enroll in St. Andrews, a private school where the teachers came from England, Ireland, Scotland and Wales. (Bob, the eldest and a teenager, returned to the United States eighteen months later to attend an American high school.)

At St. Andrews, Barbara found herself socializing by day with the Governor's daughter, the American Ambassador's daughter, children of top local government officials and very successful business leaders. After school in the evenings and on weekends she socialized with native Trinidadians from all walks of life.

After ten years in Trinidad, the family returned to the United States. Upon graduation from high school in Ottumwa, Iowa she enrolled as a freshman at Anderson College, Anderson, Indiana as music major.

Her future husband, whom she had met while living in Trinidad, was attending Kansas State University when Barbara chose to transfer during her sophomore year to KSU. During that year they became engaged and the following August were married.

Her husband's job brought them to Oklahoma where Barbara enrolled and subsequently graduated from The University of Tulsa's School of Music. The following year she joined the Broken Arrow Junior High School faculty in Broken Arrow, Oklahoma as their first full-time vocal music teacher. When her husband accepted a job with an oil company to return to Trinidad, her public school teaching career ended. As his job required, the family moved to Anaheim, California; Anchorage, Alaska and finally, to Houston, Texas.

After successfully teaching piano lessons in her own studio in Houston, Texas for thirteen years, Barbara began a small import company, Affordable Eelskin and International Fine Leather. Four years later, using the experience she had gained in the import business and the relationships she had developed with other business people throughout the country, she, along with her daughter Terrie, opened T. Carolyn in the spring of 1991. (Terrie graduated from Texas A&M University in 1987 with a Bachelor of Science in Economics and Management. Her natural talent for fashion design was recognized when several state pageant winners and a Miss USA winner wore her custom designed gowns while competing.) T. Carolyn is a ladies boutique in northwest Houston specializing in fashions for mothers of brides and grooms.

Having served as organist, pianist, vocalist and choir director at several churches through the years, Barbara had observed many weddings first hand.

Since the store opened in 1991, customers have traveled from all over the state of Texas, every state in the country, and many foreign countries to shop at T.

Carolyn. Barbara and daughter Terrie have been named the "Grande dames of fashion for mothers in Houston" by the Houston Chronicle and have established an enviable reputation among customers, manufacturers, and designers alike as foremost authorities on fashions for mothers at the wedding.

Barbara and Terrie currently hold seats on the Occasion Advisory Board for FashionCenterDallas, Dallas Apparel Mart.